D0438081

Parables
Psalms
Prayers

Sean Freeman

St. Theresa Library
Box 743
Orofino, Idaho 83544

Parables
Psalms
Prayers

Sean Freeman

THE THOMAS MORE PRESS
Chicago, Illinois

Several of the Psalms in this book appeared previously in *The Thomas More Bible Prayer Book*. Many of the Parables and Reflections were first printed in the newsletter *Markings*. The Meditations on the Rosary appeared in *Our Lady's Prayerbook*.

Copyright © 1985 by Sean Freeman. All rights reserved. Printed in the United States of America. No part of this publication may be reproduced, stored in a retrieval system, or transmitted, in any form or by any means, electronic, mechanical, photocopying, recording, or otherwise, without the written permission of the publisher, The Thomas More Association, 223 W. Erie St., Chicago, Illinois 60610.

ISBN 0-88347-185-X

Contents

PART TWO
Some Psalms Revisited

PART THREE
Prayers and Meditations on the Rosary

PART FOUR
Reflections

The characters presented in the "parables" in this book are fabrications—no resemblance to any person, alive or dead is intended.

INTRODUCTION

For those who believe, as I most ardently do, that there should be some middle way of spirituality that lies between sticky piety and playing bongo drums in sanctuaries of our churches, it is a pleasure to introduce and recommend this book.

Sean Freeman, who gave us the popular and much anthologized *The Thomas More Bible Prayer Book* some years ago, explores this middle ground of spiritual reading in ways both unconventional and traditional. His "Parables for the 80s" contain some surprising twists as well as trenchant truths. They may be taken as modern morality tales or as off-beat examples of "story theology." Some are mordant, others fraught with irony and at least one—"The Gospel for April 15th"—is just plain funny.

I must confess that with several notable exceptions, the Psalms have never yielded up to me the treasures that so many claim to have found in them down through the centuries. For my taste there is altogether too much smiting and avenging and slaying. They seem to make Yahweh more a "Godfather" in the Puzoan sense, than an all-just, all-loving Father. No less a biblical expert than John L. McKenzie admits that David—to whom many of the Psalms are attributed—seems, on balance, to have been actively pursuing the vocation of a blood-thirsty bandit.

Sean Freeman takes a highly selective journey through the Psalms and mines them for a contemporary relevance which I begrudgingly have to admit having missed. His paraphrased versions may play a little fast and loose with the original texts but, to my eye at least, they seem an improvement.

Meditating on the mysteries of the rosary may be as far out of liturgical haute couture as one can get these days, but the approach which Sean Freeman takes will be treasured by surviving devotees of the rosary—and I suspect their number could be larger than many realize.

The reflections on the major feasts and seasons of the church year which the author presents are designed to involve the reader while offering fresh insights. They are really meditations and are more rewarding read separated by intervals rather than simply rushed through at a single sitting.

This unsolicited and avuncular advice might well hold true for the book as a whole. To use a medical (or advertising) analogy, its rewards are best discovered and absorbed in small doses. So read, like a time-release capsule, it will provide many hours of relief from spiritual ennui.

Try it. You may like it.

Dan Herr

PART ONE

PARABLES FOR THE 80s

THE MODEL CHRISTIANS

On Saturday   he was lector at the evening Mass.

On Sunday   she taught CCD.

On Monday   he took credit for one of his staff member's ideas at work.

On Tuesday   she slapped her daughter's face for talking back.

On Wednesday   he attended the parish council meeting.

On Thursday   she baked brownies for the parish bake sale.

On Friday   driving home from work he grew impatient with the old lady driving the car ahead of him for not turning right on red. He honked his horn at her and watched her pull out into the path of a bread truck.

On Saturday   she called her husband a no-good drunken bum for watching the baseball game and drinking a six-pack instead of painting the kitchen as he'd promised.

On Sunday   they both went to Mass and Communion and generally felt quite good about themselves.

EVERYTHING'S UNDER CONTROL DOWN HERE

The alarm clock went off at six. Milt Thomas killed it before it woke up his wife, took his shower, shaved, dressed and went downstairs. On weekends he would have done his six miles of running first thing but Monday through Friday he worked out at the health club downtown over lunch hour and capped it off with a pre-supper jog.

He poured skimmed milk over his home-made mixture of high-fiber, sugar-free cereal, spooned it down while he listened to the weather report, then picked up his slim-line attache case and headed for the commuter station at a brisk walk to catch the 7:15. Milt, at age 56, had never felt better in his life. It paid to take care of yourself at any age but in the '50s and '60s a man had to watch out, take charge, manage his destiny. Milt had already outlived his father by three years. He had also made a lot more money than his father ever managed to accumulate through all his years of plodding routine at a job where everybody but himself had called the shots. There were no loose ends in Milt's life and he was very much in command.

His wife, no lover or appreciator of his passion for strict routine and rigorous exercise and diet programs, often told him that it was about time he relaxed and enjoyed life a bit. She, for one, was ready to kick up her heels, she said, and do some traveling and entertaining. "What good is having all this money and security and bursting vim and vigor if we don't take advantage of it? Nobody lives forever and I'd like to do a little living while I'm still able to get around without a wheelchair and a paramedic three paces behind me."

She simply didn't understand, Milt told himself as he

leaned back in his office chair. Once you let up, sit out just one round, deviate from the schedule, slip off the diet, skip the exercise, you go into a tailspin which soon lets everything get out of control.

Milt looked out his fortieth-floor window and watched the snow swirl against the enormous panes of glass. Then, humming to himself, he moved over to the computer terminal and got down to work. At 11:30 sharp his phone rang. It was Pete, right on the money, telling him he'd meet him in the lobby in five minutes. Still humming, Milt went to the closet and collected his canvas tote bag. He enjoyed Mondays at the club. Most of its members were too strung out by the excesses of their weekends to feel like showing up and sometimes he and Pete practically had the whole place, every piece of equipment, to themselves.

Milt was more than a little proud of the fact that though he was seven years older than Pete, he had no difficulty at all in matching him as an equal in anything physically competitive. He probably let it show too much because Pete, as he did this morning after they'd shaken hands in the lobby, always had some little crack prepared.

"Age before beauty," he said to Milt when they arrived simultaneously at the revolving door opening to the street. Pete stepped back and made an exaggerated flourish of deference with his arms. Milt laughed and pushed on through. It was the last thing he ever did. From a scaffold high above the entrance to the building a heavy clamp fell directly on Milt's head. He was killed instantly, dead even before he crumpled to the sidewalk in front of Pete's uncomprehending eyes.

Later in the day, when he had recovered somewhat from the shock, Pete heard himself telling a reporter, "I still can't believe it. He was here one second and gone the next. It just wasn't like Milt to let something that unexpected happen to him."

THE PRODIGAL MOTHER

As in the old nursery rhyme, there was a contemporary woman who had so many children she didn't know what to do.

Oh, she knew what to do when they were babies, and when they went off to grade school, and even—though it grew harder—when they went to high school and, some of them, to college. She fed them and washed their clothes and cleaned up after them and made their beds and nursed them when they were sick. She drove them places and comforted them and, most of all, she loved them. When the youngest of them was fourteen her husband died and she went back to work as a nurse. She knew it would be hard to work full-time and still take care of her family but she told herself they would all be moving out soon, anyway, and perhaps they would pitch in and help a little more around the house.

And sure enough, the three oldest sons soon moved to apartments. But they found their jobs were boring and it was a drag to have to buy groceries and cook and wash their own clothes and pay for their own cars and gas besides. One by one they moved back in with their mother. And she welcomed them back with open arms and very sore feet.

Her friends told her she was crazy to let them come home and to cook for them and pick up after them and wash their clothes. They told her various ways she could make their lives so miserable that they would pack up and move out for good.

But the woman just smiled and shook her head. "They are my sons," she said.

But they are grown men now, her friends explained. They are imposing on you. You have a right to a life of your own. How can you let them go on taking advantage of you like this?"

"They are only taking what I am giving," said the woman. I choose to give them the gift of myself, my love, my life. They are my sons."

And her friends went away, shaking their heads at such foolishness.

THE CHRISTMAS PRESENT

Just before midnight on Christmas Eve a man stood staring out the window of a motel office into the swirling heart of a blizzard. In a small bedroom behind the office his wife sat wrapped in blankets rocking the last hours of her life away.

"There's nothing more we can do for her," the doctor had told him when they sent her home from the hospital after the final operation and weeks of chemotherapy had failed to make any inroads on the cancer. "She's a nurse and can teach you how to give her the shots safely. It won't be for long," he added, as if that should be some sort of consolation. "At least she should make it until Christmas."

Christmas! The man didn't want to think about Christmas. All he could see was the awful dread that fluttered like bats' wings behind the pain in his wife's eyes when she looked at him, smiling, and patted his helpless hands. Whatever kind of God it was that did this to people, he wasn't about to celebrate his birthday.

Headlights barely visible, a car suddenly fish-tailed to a stop outside the window. The man was startled because he'd closed the motel weeks ago, turned off the signs and put a barricade in the drive.

Two figures struggled out of the car, the larger one supporting the smaller, and lurched up the walk to the door. "Just what I need," the man said aloud. "A lost pair of drunken holiday sheep."

But the pair turned out to be teenagers, very cold, very frightened, and the girl, very pregnant. The man considered them with distaste. Very probably they weren't even married and it was still another cruel Christmas irony that they should come to him with their unwanted child when he and his wife who had wanted children desperately had none.

"Please help us," the boy stammered. "I can't see to drive further, the car has no heater and she's in labor."

"Come in and warm up," the man said. "I will call the state police for you, but that's about all I can do. My wife is a nurse but she's dying."

The girl moaned and slid to the floor and it was obvious, even to the man, that there was no time to summon help. He motioned to the boy and together they carried her into the bedroom.

It was a long, hard birth. The boy stayed in the office, smoking. Under his wife's direction the man found himself doing things he never imagined he could do or endure. He suffered with the girl and sweated with her until at last it was over and she fell back on the pillows of the bed utterly spent.

When he placed the tiny boy, glistening and wet in his wife's blanketing arms she said, so softly that he could scarcely hear her, "Thank you."

Her eyes grew enormous and bright as any star. The black wings of dread dissolved and the man, peering into them through his own tears, could see absolutely nothing there but love.

THE GOSPEL FOR APRIL 15th
(Matthew 21; IRS 1040)

"Then the Pharisees went away and agreed on a plan to trap him in his own words. Some of their followers were sent to him in the company of men of Herod's party. They said, 'Master, you are an honest man, we know; you teach in all honesty the way of life that God requires, fearing no man, whoever he may be. Give us then your ruling on this: is it lawful for us to pay taxes to Caesar?' Jesus was aware of their wicked intentions and said to them, 'You hypocrites! Why are you trying to catch me out? Show me the money in which the tax is paid.' They handed him a piece of silver. Jesus asked, 'Is this a long term or a short term capital gain? What is your filing status? Did you deduct expenses for an office in your home? Did you or any member of your family use your vacation home for more than two weeks this year? Did you use an Accelerated Cost Recovery System for depreciation?'

"Hearing all this they despaired and went away and hanged themselves on a Privacy and Paperwork Reduction Act Notice."

YOUR OLD MEN SHALL DREAM DREAMS
Joel 2:28

The nurse rolled Mr. Tobin's wheelchair onto the terrace of the nursing home and then walked over to join the cook who was sitting on one of the steps smoking a cigarette.

"How's the vegetable today?" the cook asked. "What with all this nice spring sunshine maybe you should water him down good and see if anything sprouts."

"It's a waste," replied the nurse. "He just sits there taking up space and my time. He hasn't said anything in three years and aside from an occasional twitch he doesn't move anything but his bowels and his mouth when I cram the food in. At least he doesn't complain about your cooking the way all the rest of them do. Twelve hundred a month it costs his son—what a lot of living I could do with that kind of money. And the doctor says he could last for years, even if he is closing in on 90."

Mr. Tobin, whose hearing was quite acute, stopped listening to them and tuned in the chirping of the goldfinches in the honeysuckle bush, which was just on the verge of blooming. The sun felt delicious on the back of his neck and the air was so perfect he wished he could bottle it up and save it to breathe back in the stuffy room with the nonopening windows where they kept him since his last stroke.

He didn't blame his son for putting him in the home. The nurse was right, he was a vegetable—at least his body was. But no turnip ever dreamed the dreams that he did, no carrot reveled in the total recall he had discovered in his aging but, to him, miraculous brain. For in the last three years, deprived of virtually every physical function, Mr. Tobin had learned how to travel in his head, how to mine the riches of a past he had evidently been too busy to appreciate while he had been living it. All he had to do was close his eyes and . . . .

It was a soft summer evening in 1926. He parked the mud-spattered Ford on a tiny patch of gravel just off the dirt road and swayed across the rope footbridge which spanned the boulder-studded creek that roared down from the misty flanks of the mountains all around him. He turned left and followed the steep trail back up the creek, feeling the fine spray that made the jungle of rhododendrons glisten cool his forehead and wash away the tensions of another day's struggle to carve a few hundred more feet of highway through the Great Smokey Mountain National Park.

Creek and path veered sharply right and he saw her forty yards upstream balanced precariously on a rock, casting into a deep pool. She stood in profile to him, a theatrical shaft of fading sunlight making a bronze nimbus of her hair. She was impossibly slender and worked the fly rod as if it were an extension of her own lithe arm just as he had taught her to. They had been married for nearly three months but her beauty still shocked him. Coming upon her in this dripping green wilderness seemed utterly unreal. Hardnosed young engineers were not supposed to admit to such feelings, but she made his heart sing.

As he moved on up the path, in considerable peril now because he refused to take his eyes off her even to check his footing, he saw her rod bow and the line rip taut. She fought the trout too hard but managed to work it closer and closer to the rock.

The roar of the creek deafened her to his approach and he could have sworn that she hadn't seen him, but when she rose from her teetering crouch, gleaming fish in hand, she turned toward him, radiantly victorious and totally unsurprised and said, "Here's your supper."

He kissed her lightly, took the flyrod in one hand and her arm in the other and began climbing up toward the cabin which clung to the ridge above the creek . . . .

That was as good a spot as any, so Mr. Tobin simply froze the moment in his mind and stayed in it.

"Look at him," said the nurse. "If I didn't know better I'd say he was smiling—probably just a gas pain."

"Not from my food," the cook said laughing. "Maybe the old codger is still alive and kicking in there somewhere. Maybe he's even happy."

"You bet," the nurse snorted, "and maybe you'd like to change places with him."

In one of his increasingly rare moments of frustration, Mr. Tobin wished he could talk again, just long enough to yell, "Not on your life!"

VACANCY

George Allenby stood in the lobby of the motel with nothing but question marks dancing in front of his eyes. It must be another one of those momentary lapses he'd been experiencing of late, because the last thing he remembered was being in his car on the interstate.

The rain had been slashing down and he distinctly recalled thinking that if his wife had been with him she would have been mumbling some of those silly prayers of hers. George wasn't the praying type—there was nobody up there listening as far as he was concerned—but he had admitted that if it got much worse he would have to pull off and stop. Which is what he must have done and why he was standing here, safe and sound, in a motel he couldn't remember entering. But he hated these damnable memory lapses which left him totally disoriented and very much out of touch with himself and probably looking very foolish, indeed.

He glanced at his watch but it had evidently suffered a lapse of its own and stopped. He looked around the lobby but couldn't see a clock anywhere. He felt totally whacked out and, while he couldn't find any windows to confirm it, he was certain that it was still pouring. The smart thing to do would be to register for the night if there was still a room to be had, call his wife, have a quick one at the bar and go to bed.

The young lady at the registration desk was extraordinarily beautiful. Not just attractive, or pretty but luminously gorgeous, with a face like the photographs of the young Greta Garbo George so much admired. No one else was to be seen, however.

Practically tongue-tied by the girl's beauty, George was further dazzled by the warmth of her smile when she responded to his garbled inquiry by saying, "Of course Mr. Allenby, we've been expecting you."

She handed him a key attached to a heavy brass medallion. "Just go down the hall to your right—room 109—about halfway along. I'm sure you'll find everything to your liking. If you need anything just give me a call."

"Don't you want me to fill out a card or anything," George mumbled. "I have every kind of plastic there is."

"That won't be necessary," the girl told him brightly, "we know your credit rating is tops, Mr. Allenby."

Amazing, George thought, they must have some kind of scanner and computer which got all sorts of data by instant tracing of your license plate number right from the parking lot.

"I'm sure the restaurant is closed," George said with some of his old authority (he was pleased to be recognized and valued for the solid citizen that he was), "but is it possible to get anything from room service? Also, I have to make a long distance call to my wife."

"Oh, your wife knows that you're here, Mr. Allenby—or she will in a few minutes. But I'm afraid that we don't have room service, or a restaurant, for that matter. She favored him with another Garboesque smile, but there was a definite message of dismissal in this one.

Faint alarm bells began to go off in George's mind. No one admired the wonders of the electronic age more than he did but was there really a machine that read license plates in rain-swept parking lots, checked your credit rating and marital status and then called your wife? A lot of men he knew damn well didn't want their wives to know when they checked into a motel.

Something very fishy was going on here. No clocks, no people, no registration, no restaurant, no bar, and a desk clerk who could be making $200 an hour modelling. And the scariest thing of all was that George suddenly realized that, whereas a minute ago he'd been dying for a drink and lusting for the medically forbidden delights of a greasy cheeseburger all topped off with a nice contraband cigar he suddenly had no interest in, much less craving for, any of these things.

As he started down the hall to find the room, it dawned on George that he had no luggage—no toothbrush, no comb or brush, no change of clothes—nothing but his car keys and a wallet full of credit cards this crazy motel had no interest in.

Room 109 was on the right. The door was ajar and the lights on. It was large and furnished in a style which was distinctly elegant but also extremely simple—soft blue walls with recessed niches holding lamps and some vaguely classic-looking statuettes which George didn't recognize. There were several ultra-modern free-form lounges scattered about, all covered in the same soft dusty gold fabric.

Pleasant enough, George thought—and then it hit him. There was no bed in this room. There was no bathroom that he could find. There was no chest of drawers, no television set—not even a black-and-white. There were no closets, no tables, no luggage stand.

No wonder they didn't need a registration card filled out, George thought, outraged now, but also fighting panic. This was no motel room—it was more like a . . . waiting room. Yes, a waiting room, a reception area. One of the niches held a telephone. George marched over to it, all his complaints ready to boil over.

Just as he reached for the phone it rang. George drew back his hand as from a hissing snake. The phone rang again—louder, this time, it seemed to George. He picked it up. The dulcet voice of the girl at the desk said, "I have a call for you Mr. Allenby, a very special call."

Martha, thought George, it's got to be Martha wanting to see what the hell I'm doing in this place. I don't blame her, probably scared to death being called by some computer in the middle of the night.

"Hi honey!" George said, "I was just about to call you . . ."

"Don't you honey me, George Allenby" . . . . The very words George had expected to hear but disconcertingly, catastrophically, it was not his wife's voice that said them. A very, very familiar voice, but definitely not Martha's.

"Now you've gotten yourself into a pretty pickle, haven't you?" George's memory, working at lightning speed came up with the correct identity of the caller but his conscious mind refused to accept it.

"You got so smart, so sophisticated . . . forgot everything I taught you to believe in . . . . Well you'd better start believing it now and fast. I've got some influence here or you wouldn't be where you are right now but it's just for a matter of minutes and you were never really very quick, George, in spite of all the money you've made. Try to think now, George. Really try. Nobody can do it but you and you'd better not fool yourself this time."

No doubt about it. It simply couldn't be but it definitely was.

"Mother!" George blurted in a strangled voice. He was

suddenly afflicted with a terrible vision of his mother as he'd last seen her, lying in the open casket but holding a phone to her waxed red lips.

He shouted into the phone again but the line was dead. George hung up and slumped down on one of the lounges, his mind reeling. He must now be afflicted with hallucinations as well as memory lapses—or perhaps this whole thing was a dream. But he disposed of this comforting possibility by squeezing the room key tightly until the pain was unbearable. He turned over the key's medallion to read the name of the motel. There was nothing but the room number and the single etched word PENDING.

Pending—pending what? George went back over his mother's words, trying to piece them together from the muddle of his shock. He was to think about something, decide on something, remember something he used to believe in, something his mother had taught him. But for the life of him, George couldn't imagine what she was babbling about, even if he accepted the preposterous notion that it had been his mother talking in the first place.

To hell with this! Rain or no rain, George decided that he was going to check out of this looney bin, get back in his car and drive home.

He got up and moved toward the door, halfway expecting it to have been locked from the outside by the beautiful kook from the desk. The door held a full-length mirror but it wasn't until George turned the handle and began—to his immense relief—to pull it open that he noticed it: a perfectly ordinary plate glass mirror with beveled edges into which George stared with horror. The mirror reflected the softly lighted room behind him, the lounges, even the key in his hand—but it was not reflecting him.

Like a child with a Fourth of July sparkler, George swung the key's medallion in arcs and slashes, watching the glinting patterns it produced in the mirror. This just cannot be, George told himself. I'm here but I'm not here.

The realization came down on him inexorably, like an icy fog, insinuating itself around his every rationalization and outraged objection. He'd been in an accident. He'd been killed. He was dead—as dead as his mother.

But dead people don't check into motels and talk on telephones. When you're dead, you're dead. Until this instant George had been as sure of that as he had been that all the religious twaddle that his mother and Martha and thousands like them believed was so much hopeful pie in the sky. What if it was true after all? Was that what his mother had been trying to tell him? If it was, then he was in very big trouble indeed.

George began to sob convulsively. He was wracked by tremors and spasms of self-pity. The room key fell silently to the carpet in front of the vacant mirror. George sucked in air in great gasps. Words formed themselves in his throat and forced themselves out of his mouth in a scream.

"Oh my God!"

The room was still reverberating when the phone rang again—a booming, gong-like intonation that stilled George's spasms and made him go rigid with fear. It sounded again, commandingly, and George approached it like a robot, picking up the receiver with a jerky motion and holding it to his throbbing ear.

A voice to which George's heart responded with an immense leap of joy said simply—"Yes?"

BIRTH OF A SALESMAN

In the early afternoon the canopied catamaran launch left
the side of the cruise ship and headed toward one of An-
tigua's perfect beaches. The boat was filled with American
tourists, a group of award-winning insurance salesmen and
their wives, who slurped away at the first of the free pina
coladas dispensed from the well-stocked bar and strained
their ears for the faint sounds of the steel band which was
already serenading them from the shore.

For a while the tourists had the beach to themselves. They
splashed and swam and a few of the more adventurous put
on face masks and snorkled around the fringes of a small
reef. They grew red and boisterous in the sun and retreated
often to the shade of the launch's awning for another exotic
drink.

But the music and laughter soon attracted a swarm of vendors, mostly young men and boys, who descended on the
tourists with basketwork, scarves, cheap jewelry and packets
of island-grown spices. At first, the tourists tolerated their
pushing clamor with amused good grace but as the afternoon
wore on and the vendors grew more numerous and persis-
tent, their mood grew irritable and they began complaining
to one another and finally to the boat's crew that it was time
to return to the ship.

"Unspoiled island paradise, my foot," complained one
woman to her husband. "These kids are all over us no matter where we go, thick as flies and twice as pesky."

When they saw that the launch was preparing to leave, the
vendors grew positively frenzied, practically forcing their
wares into the tourists' hands. Finally, they gave up and

retreated, all but one very small boy who waded out into the water with a packet of spices and waved it toward the woman's husband.

"Please, mister," he said with tears running down his cheeks, "I have sold nothing at all for the whole day—I give you all these fine things for just two dollars."

The man was moved and in spite of knowing that he had nothing but a ten-dollar bill in his wallet, handed it out to the child and took the spices.

The boy's face cracked wide with pleasure.

"I will bring you change, good mister," he shouted and struggled back up into the crowd on the beach.

"What on earth possessed you to do that?" his wife demanded. "You know you'll never see any change from that and these spices are soaked in sea water."

"I know," said the man, "but he reminded me of how I felt when I made my very first sale, after peddling door to door for a week, to a woman who, I'm sure, bought something she didn't need, just because she saw the desperation in my face."

The catamaran had swung about now, well clear of the beach, and was moving slowly toward the ship. The husband and wife sat down in the stern and watched the steel band load their instruments onto a rusty old pick-up truck.

The husband heard splashing and looked down to see a small brown hand gripping the edge of the boat's deck. In an instant its twin appeared and slapped eight thoroughly soggy dollar bills at his feet.

THE URBAN SAMARITANS

On Sunday morning as they were leaving their high-rise apartment to walk to Mass at the Cathedral, Mrs. Brown asked her husband if he had remembered to write the check for the Catholic Charities collection.

"I did," said Mr. Brown, "but it's not as much as we gave last year. I've been reading about some of the wacko organizations that get the money."

The Cathedral was old and, though only a few blocks from the Browns' luxury apartment building, not in the best of neighborhoods. The Browns would have preferred to drive their Mercedes but it was too risky to leave it parked on the street, even for an hour on Sunday morning.

"We're going to be late," said Mrs. Brown as they waited for a three-way light to say "Walk." Just as it did, an old lady next to them tripped on the curbing and went sprawling. She bloodied her knees and hit her head. She lay there moaning.

Mr. Brown moved toward her.

"Don't you try to help her up," Mrs. Brown ordered. "You move these people and they sue you for fake injuries," she said. "Besides you know you've got a bad back and you're bound to get blood on your new suit. Let the paramedics help her."

By this time two other people were leaning over the old lady so the Browns moved on—though they had to wait for the light to change again.

In the middle of the next block they were approached by a seedy-looking character who actually had the nerve to block their way. He didn't say anything, just stuck a scabby, filthy hand palm-up at Mr. Brown's chest. Mr. Brown put his hand in his pocket and fumbled for some change.

"You get out of our way at once or I'll call a policeman," Mrs. Brown told the man angrily. "Why should we give you any of our hard-earned money to spend on cheap wine. There's nothing wrong with you. Go get a job and work like the rest of us."

The man called Mrs. Brown a dirty name but he got out of the way.

"This walk is getting impossible," said Mrs. Brown as they climbed the Cathedral steps. "From now on we're going to take a cab."

Mrs. Brown's first prediction was right. They were indeed late. The priest was already reading the Gospel as they walked up the side aisle:

" . . . 'And who is my neighbor?' Jesus replied, 'A man was on his way from Jerusalem down to Jericho when he fell in with robbers; they stripped him, beat him and went off leaving him half dead . . . .' "

THE MASS-GOER
(Liturgy for any Sunday of the year)

Let us pray.

"He's got nerve showing his face here after the divorce. I wonder if he'll try to go to Communion."

"What makes her think she's a lector. Voice like an asthmatic cat, and that outfit she's got on!"

"These readings and responses are pointless. Who cares about a bunch of Jews wandering around in the desert?"

"Oh, no! Not another twenty-minute special by young Father Know-it-all. He preaches more politics than religion —peace, poverty, racial justice—his needle's stuck."

"Two collections again! If that inner-city parish can't hack it let them close up shop. There's not a Catholic in a carload down there anyway."

"All this singing drives me batty. Makes me feel like I'm back in kindergarten."

"Here we go again. Kiss-of-peace-phoney-smile-limp-hand-shake-time. Worse than the Rotary Club."

"If they think I'm going to take Communion from an insurance salesman they're crazy. I'll just move over to the main aisle."

"Yes, I knew it. There he is receiving—bold as brass."

"How do they expect anybody to go in peace when they play a recessional like that—more like a barn dance."

"Well, at least it's over for another week. Now if I can avoid the pastor on the way out."

Amen.

MS. MERRICK'S LAST CCD CLASS

"Well, children, I'm sorry to have to say that this is the last Sunday morning we'll be spending together. The pastor, upon recommendations from the committee and your other teachers, has asked me to resign because I have not stuck conscientiously to the lesson plan prescribed for us. They say that I'm confusing you dangerously and filling your heads with radical ideas. Perhaps I am. Anyway, for our final scripture lesson, I'm going to read you the following passage and then we'll discuss it.

THE SERMON ON MOUNT CHAUVINIST

When he saw the crowds he went up the hill. There he sat down and when his disciples had gathered around him he began to address them. And this is the teaching he gave:

"Since the time of Eve, women have been the seat of temptation and the undoing of men. Not all women are evil but it is their very nature to entice and distract. Therefore they can be admitted to my church but should remain silent therein. They may adorn and scrub the altar but never preach. Much less may they aspire to the priestly role because as the Father is male, and I am male, so must all my priests be male. And they must be content in their lot and not expect to have a voice proportionate with their numbers or their service.

"Yea, I say verily that there will come a time when the daughters of Eve will clamor for these forbidden things and offer affronts and protests even unto the highest of priests and in the holiest of holies. But the blessed among them will see the errors of these ways and by their docile demeanor shame their strident sisters into silence. Let them take my mother, meek and mild, as their example. For it is written, and I give it now to you again, that woman's place is in the home and in the pew, and thus must it ever be."

"Ms. Merrick, did Jesus really say that?"

"No, Julia, he did not."

"Is it really in the Bible?"

"No, Sandra, it is not."

"Then why did you read it to us?"

"You'll find out."

THE LOVING DAUGHTER

A certain couple had one child, a daughter. She was, quite naturally, the focus of all their love and concern. Nothing was too good for their daughter. Even though they were not prosperous, they somehow managed to see that she had fine clothes and was educated at the best of schools. In every way they taught and showed her that she was a very special person.

And the daughter returned her parents' love. Even after she had married—quite well, indeed, to a successful surgeon —and moved to another town, and had two children of her own to care for, she continued to write and call and visit them whenever she could manage. This was, of course, not very frequently. Her husband worked long hours and on many weekends, so she involved herself in volunteer work. She visited elderly people in nursing homes and worked on the community's commission on aging.

When her parents finally complained that they really would like to see more of their grandchildren—and their daughter—hinting broadly that if she could not come to them, they could now manage some extended visits of their own, she told them that while she would love nothing more, her schedule was such that it wouldn't be practical just now.

To offset their disappointment she showered the parents with expensive gifts at Christmas and even offered, with her husband's blessing, to send them on a world cruise. But on the Friday after Christmas her father died.

At the funeral the daughter noticed for the first time how old her mother had grown and her heart was filled with pity.

She arranged for her mother to sell the family house and move in with her at once.

But away from her home and friends, stripped of her husband's love and companionship, the mother became self-pitying and possessive. She insisted on being part of the daughter's social life. She cooked great quantities of food which neither the daughter's children nor husband would touch. She even intruded upon the few precious hours of privacy the daughter and her husband could manage.

And soon the mother's health began to fail. She seemed to need constant attention. She would look at her daughter and burst into tears for no reason. She was resented by the children who found her an embarrassment when their friends came to visit. In short, for such a very special person as the daughter knew herself to be, her mother was an impossible burden.

"It's not fair," she told herself. "It is not my fault that I am an only child so that the total burden of caring for my mother must fall on me." And her husband, tiring of the endless tension in his home, agreed.

Through her connections the daughter had no trouble placing her mother in the very best of nursing homes, where she visited her faithfully every Sunday morning—which, given the daughter's schedule, was quite a sacrifice—for the next eight years until the mother died.

THE PARISH TROUBLEMAKER

"Is she here again?" asked the President of the Parish Council.

"In the very last row wearing her frumpy parka, as usual," said the recording secretary.

The meeting came to order.

"We finally have the funds to pave the parking lot," the President announced.

"The Brannigan's house burned down. They have no insurance and he's out of work," said the lady in the last row.

"That's tragic," replied the President, "but it's not what we're here to discuss. The contractor wants $2,000 deposit before . . ."

"I know three families whose heat has been turned off because they can't pay their gas bills," the lady in the back row announced.

" . . . before he begins but he'll throw in the rectory driveway free," the President continued.

"Last year the Council pledged $500 to stock an 'open parish pantry' for the needy," said the lady in the last row, standing up and pointing her finger at the podium, "when extra funds became available. Why can't we just put some more gravel on the parking lot and use the difference to help people?"

Everyone turned and glared at the lady in the last row.

"Helping people is not what this meeting is about," the President told her. "Helping people is a wonderful thing but it is not the purpose of the Parish Council. We have an organization to run here, a parish plant to maintain. We cannot achieve these goals with people like you disrupting every meeting. You are out of order and if you don't sit down and be quiet I'm going to have to ask you to leave."

The audience applauded the President.

The lady in back row zipped up her parka, picked up her two shopping bags and headed for the door.

"I'll be back next month," she said. "Maybe by then you will have changed your minds."

THE RESPECTABLE FATHER

There was a successful businessman in Milwaukee who was
a pillar of church and community. One year he headed both
his parish's building drive and the city's United Way campaign. With his large family he attended Mass each Sunday
and was selected to be an extraordinary minister of the
Eucharist.

He was a model husband, ever faithful, and a just and loving father who told his children that no matter what troubles
they might fall into they should turn first to him for help.
But beyond a few traffic arrests and minor disciplinary
scrapes at school, none of his children presented him with
any serious problems. Indeed, people often asked him what
secrets of parenthood he and his wife practiced that their
children, virtually alone among their peers, resisted or eluded
the adolescent pitfalls of drugs and drink and promiscuity.

"No secret," the father said. "I tell them that virtue earns
its own rewards, especially in terms of respect. Self-respect
and the respect of others. They are my children and they
have an image to maintain. When they let themselves down
they are letting me down, as well. Without respect we are
nothing in the eyes of man or God."

His eldest child, a daughter, went away to college. In her
second semester she fell in love with a married professor and
became pregnant. The professor told her that much as he
loved her he could not risk the scandal of a divorce. He
would, however, both arrange and pay for an abortion.

The daughter, recalling her father's pledge of help in time
of trouble, phoned him and confessed her predicament. She
said that she knew that abortion was as much against his

principles as hers and that she wanted to return home, have the baby, put it up for adoption in the city, and then return to her studies at another college.

"NO," said the father. "It cannot be. Your presence here would give grave scandal. It would appear to your brothers and sisters, and to the community that I was sanctioning your wanton behavior. You have let yourself down and you have let me down. I will not allow you to destroy the respect of our family. It is true that I am against abortion but that is your problem and not mine to wrestle with. All I can tell you is that we do not wish to see you here pregnant and unmarried."

The daughter pondered all this in her heart, grew bitter and despaired. "It appears that both my father and the professor love respect more than they love me—they love it even more than life."

So the next morning the daughter called the *Milwaukee Journal*, gave her name and explained what she about to do and why. Then she took a gun, entered the professor's classroom and killed herself.

TWELVE THINGS TO GIVE UP FOR LENT

Having to have the last word.

Taking those you love for granted.

Worrying about things you cannot change or control.

Losing your temper.

Trying to be a perfectionist.

Patronizing people who work for or with you.

Complaining.

Carrying grudges.

Expecting to be bored by any and all sermons.

Nagging.

Thinking about money.

Feeling sorry for yourself.

THE HIGH COST OF LOVING

Mr. Timmons was a meticulous man. He was also very frugal. By nature and profession he was an accountant—a most successful one. He had three favorite sayings:

> "A place for everything, and everything in its place."

> "Don't put your heart and your money in the same pocket."

> "There is no such thing as a free lunch."

Mr. Timmons and his wife had one child, a son, and Mr. Timmons worked constantly to instill the wisdom contained in his three pet sayings in his wife and son. He wanted them to know the value of money and the satisfying geometry of order and thrift.

After a few years, Mrs. Timmons expressed a wish to have more children, but Mr. Timmons wisely pointed out to her that raising a brood of children in the inflationary economy of the day was a terribly expensive proposition, one which most parents, blinded by rash and romantic instincts, failed to comprehend. To drive home his point Mr. Timmons showed his wife a ledger which he had opened the day their son had been born. It showed every expenditure incurred on his behalf from the hospital to a crib, diapers, baby food, clothes and doctors' bills. Even now, when the child was only four, the total amounted to several thousand dollars.

"And that's just the tip of the iceberg," he told his wife.

Mr. Timmons was right, of course. By the time the son

was eighteen, even allowing for Mr. Timmons frugal management, the ledger total stood at over $45,000. When the son had finished college and gotten an advanced degree in business, the ledger stood at a staggering $82,000.

On his son's wedding day, Mr. Timmons took the young man aside and showed him the ledger.

"This is my wedding present to you," he told him. "Think about it when you plan the size of your own family. As you can see, a child is not exactly 'a gift of God.'"

The young couple moved off to California where the son worked hard and well and soon founded his own highly profitable electronics company. After five years they had two children who became the apples of his parents' eyes. In fact, Mr. Timmons, who found himself mellowing a bit with age, not only showered them with lavish gifts but soon decided to take an early retirement so that he and his wife could move to California to be closer to the grandchildren.

When he, excited, called to tell his son this news the young man told him to hold on, that he was making a special trip home—alone—to settle a vital piece of outstanding business.

He arrived at his parents' house the following Saturday. Opening his briefcase, he took out an envelope and handed it to his father.

"This is a check payable to you in the amount of $118,900. It covers the $82,000 shown in the ledger you gave me, plus five years interest at nine percent. I have paid in full for my 'free lunch' and I never want to see you again in my life. Goodbye."

WOULD MOTHER TERESA TAKE A TAXI?

As he grew older Mr. Ainsley found himself rising earlier and earlier each morning. A bachelor, he had no one's routine to conform to but his own, so he began going to work at the newspaper (where he was a veteran editor and Pulitzer Prize-winning columnist) soon after he got up. He did some of his best writing early in the day and the newspaper offices never closed.

Some of his colleagues warned him that walking the city streets at six on dark winter mornings was not the safest form of urban exercise and that if he insisted on coming to the office at that hour he should take a cab.

But Mr. Ainsley, who had been a champion of civil rights and social justice for minorities long before either cause became popular with "neo-liberals," as he called them, simply responded with one of his well-known outraged snorts and told them they were a bunch of lily-livered alarmists.

"The day I'm afraid to walk to work in this town is the day I should quit," he muttered fiercely. Secretly, Mr. Ainsley felt that his reputation and recognizability would protect him—anyone who read the paper or watched television would know him for the good guy that he was. The very notion of any black or Latino street tough mugging him was as unthinkable as English peasants turning on Robin Hood, or a native of Calcutta beating up on Mother Teresa.

So it came as a trauma to his self-image when, one dark and swirling December morning, Mr. Ainsley, halfway between his apartment and the office, suddenly became aware of a prickling sensation at the base of his neck. He was in the middle of a long block occupied by the main post office which loomed solidly upward on his right. Ahead, two large black men came briskly toward him. This in itself did not bother him but today he was a full half-hour earlier than he'd ever been on this block. And now another man seemed to be coming at him diagonally from across the street. He stopped and looked back. Still another was coming on him from the rear.

In spite of the bitter cold, Mr. Ainsley began to sweat.

"I will not panic," he told himself even as he began to do so. There could be no doubt of it now. All of these men were definitely converging on him and he doubted very much if they wanted his autograph.

Mr. Ainsley's physical condition was such that he was long past sprinting, even if there had been some place to run. He simply stood there and let fear and hate and self-pity take him over.

The four men—looking enormous and absolutely brutal —were almost on him.

"Savages!" thought Mr. Ainsley as he crouched instinctively and covered his head with his arms. The man from behind actually brushed past him.

"Hey, man," he asked, "you all right?"

Mr. Ainsley peered cautiously out between his crossed forearms. There was a sudden outpouring of light as a door opened and the three other men entered the post office.

"I'm O.K. now," Mr. Ainsley told the man who had spoken to him.

"You sure?" the man said. "Old guy like you got no business out in these mean streets so early."

"My God," Mr. Ainsley asked himself as he walked unsteadily on toward the newspaper office, "what kind of person am I?"

He had a lot to sort out, that was for sure, but whether or not one instance of panic, hatred and falsely perceived threat made him a hypocritical bigot, the postal worker was right: an old guy like him had no business out on the mean streets so early.

TONGUES OF FIRE
Class Notes from a Meeting of Christian Humanity 101

Professor Thomas: The title of Nobel Prize-winner Saul Bellow's most recent book is *Him With His Foot in His Mouth*. The lead story is about a man—an academic type —who all his life has been unable to resist making what Dorothy Parker called "smart cracks."

In his old age he abandons his life-long atheism in favor of a sort of hopeful agnosticism—he is willing, like Pascal, to accept the bet, the wager, that there just might possibly be a God and, if so, he realizes he has nothing to lose and everything to gain by straightening out his earthly affairs as best he can. If indeed this Christian-Judaic God exists, rumor and tradition have it that he puts a lot of stock in charity, in loving one's fellow human beings. And the professor is acutely conscious that his addiction to smartcracking has caused him to sin outrageously against that very virtue.

As the story opens he is writing a letter of apology to one of his early victims, a lady who, years ago, had been one of his students. Through a mutual acquaintance the professor has learned that something he said to the then young woman shook her confidence and profoundly wounded her self-image.

It seems that one day when the professor was passing the library wearing a baseball cap the young woman spotted him and, startled by this unexpectedly sportive headgear atop one of her demigods, blurted out: "Oh Dr. Shawmut, in that cap you look like an archeologist." Unable to stop himself, the professor cracked back: "And you look like something I just dug up."

The young woman may have been too sensitive by far to let such a barb so blight her life, but the young are especially vulnerable. Socialite Diana Vreeland recalls in her autobiography a verbal wound which her own mother inflicted on her when she was very small: "It's too bad that you have such a beautiful sister and that you are so extremely ugly and so terribly jealous of her."

We all need to think before we talk, to pass our words through a "final filter" that measures their potential impact on the ears they are intended for. Children wound each other with words out of spite or just plain thoughtlessness—"You have the biggest nose I've ever seen!" "Are your eyes always crossed like that?"—but adults should know and speak better. I'm certain that everybody in the class has been on the receiving end of a barb, or jibe, or thoughtless crack that has haunted them all their life. At the same time, I'm almost certain that we have all been guilty of delivering one or more such life-time zingers to others.

And while we are examining our consciences let's also resolve to expurgate from our unthinking repertoire all those platitudinous phrases of sympathy which we lay on people who have just suffered a loss or trauma: "It's a blessing that he didn't go on suffering longer than he did." "It must be a relief that it's finally over." "I know you are hurt by the divorce but, confidentially, I never did really understand what you saw in her." "I know lots of people who have beaten cancer like yours." Far better just to give an embrace or a handshake of silent sympathy or, if you must say something: "You must be going through hell."

Even those professional wits, famous for their quips, often live to regret them. In New York the young and beautiful

Clare Boothe was building a reputation for her quick and caustic wit. But she met her match the day she ran into the previously mentioned Dorothy Parker at the entrance to a fashionable dinner club. Miss Parker was older than Miss Boothe who stepped aside and with a flourish waved Parker through the door with the words: "Age before beauty." And Parker swept through ahead of her saying, ever so sweetly, "Pearls before swine."

Now are there any questions or comments?
Yes, Sally.

Sally: Professor Thomas, do you always lisp when you give an especially dull lecture?

SEE HOW THE RIGHTEOUS SUFFER

To her way of thinking—and anyone who really knew the situation at St. Anselm's would have to agree—Margaret Cawley really ran the parish. The practical side of things, that is. The aging pastor, Father Malachy, was a pious man, to be sure, beloved by young and old, but about as effective as a limp noodle when it came to administration and money. And the assistant, or as he liked to think of himself, the associate pastor, Father Meeger, she called "Saint Elsewhere," because he never seemed to be around the rectory long enough to tend to business. He was totally wrapped up in one or another of his "peace and justice" causes, or in taking theology courses with long names at the local college.

St. Anselm's school had long since closed its doors and all the nuns disappeared into the secular hinterland, so it was left to Margaret, as the only concerned parishioner with enough gumption and know-how, to see to everything from the Altar and Rosary Society to the annual benefit to rounding up altar boys, ushers and lectors—and a lot more beside.

The pastor was wise enough to let her run things in her own efficient way, but his housekeeper, Agnes Foley, an inept and sickly soul, was clearly jealous of Margaret and did everything she could to snarl things up. At least a half-dozen times a week she failed to deliver an important message from Margaret to the pastor or, worse, would simply refuse to tell him that Margaret was on the phone. "Father is saying his Office now and can't be disturbed," she would say in her snuffy voice. Or, "Father's resting now—just give me the message and I'll see that he gets it." But she didn't, of course, so Margaret would have to call back—sometimes 15 or 20 times a day.

Besides all this, Agnes was a classic hypochondriac who ran off to the doctor every time she felt a twinge, incurring steep medical bills which the parish could certainly not afford. It finally became clear to Margaret that the woman simply had to go—a decision she put to the pastor in no uncertain terms.

"Ah," he responded, "but Agnes is really a good woman who has served the parish loyally for all these many years. We cannot simply dump her out into the street now, can we?"

Deeply hurt by the pastor's defiance and obvious lack of appreciation for all she had done, Margaret decided to teach him a lesson. If he valued his precious Agnes so much, just let him depend solely on her for a while. She would simply drop out of the picture for a few weeks and see how he liked it.

But the very next day Margaret herself fell ill—gall bladder, and it called for surgery. For three long days after her operation she lay in her hospital room waiting for a visit from the pastor or at least Saint Elsewhere. Finally, late on the fourth day, Father Malachy appeared at her bedside. He looked drawn and weary.

"I'm terribly sorry not to have gotten here sooner," he told Margaret, "but Agnes was brought here the same day you were and I've spent a great deal of time with her."

In spite of herself, tears welled up in Margaret's eyes— whether from fury or self-pity she didn't know.

"Oh, don't concern yourself with me or my suffering," she hissed. "You must hurry back to her. What's she complaining of this time? A rash? Or is it her back acting up on her again?"

"Agnes died a few minutes ago," Father Malachy told her. "She had been fighting cancer for the past two years but didn't want anybody to know and feel sorry for her. She left you this note."

Margaret tore open the envelope he gave her and read: "Dear Margaret, forgive me for all the times I let you down. You are the sort of person I always wanted to be. Get well soon, the parish needs you. Peace, Agnes."

Margaret handed the note to Father Malachy and began to cry again. But this time she knew exactly why.

PART TWO

SOME PSALMS REVISITED

Lord, I know that we are to bear adversity for your sake.

But I am weak and I ask your merciful help in this trial.

For it is tormenting me beyond bearing.

How long, O Lord, how long must I bear it?

I am consumed by anguish

so that my days are made useless by worry

and my nights filled with sleepless tossing.

You are my only hope.

Hear my prayer and help me.

Psalm 6

Not nearly as often as I should,

I sometimes stop to reflect on your great goodness.

When I consider the moon and the stars

and the unknown depths of the universe,

the insignificance of man,

the insignificance of me,

become apparent.

Who am I that you should care for me?

Yet here we are, made in your image,

a little less than the angels.

You have given us the world

and mastery over it.

You have given us this life

and promised another that will not end.

I wonder at your goodness.

Forgive me if I forget it tomorrow.

Psalm 8

"God save us! There are no honest people left.
Fidelity seems to have vanished from the earth.
All I hear are lies, flattery, doubletalk."

Psalm 12

How nice it is to know that things haven't changed.

What a testimony to the enduring weakness
of human nature!

Of course there are some good people around today.

Let's see . . . there's you and I.

That makes two, I think.

Lord who is truly righteous?

"The person who leads a blameless life.

Who does right always.

Who speaks the truth.

Who does not slander others.

Who refuses to harm others.

Who never blames his neighbor.

Who stands faithfully by her word.

Who takes advantage of no one.

Who has compassion on the poor.

The person who does all these things
is truly righteous in my eyes."

Psalm 15

"The heavens manifest the glory of God.
The vast reaches of space are filled with his presence.
Each new day proclaims his glory.
Each night confirms it anew."

Psalm 19

Sometimes, when I am overfilled with the words
of theologians,

befuddled by their jargon,

confounded by their distinctions,

alarmed by their reservations,

Sometimes, when belief seems a complex operation,

too tricky by half for me to master,

Sometimes when doubts assail me

(What's a nice nuclear age person like me doing
in a faith like this?)

Sometimes, when I feel like that,

I take a walk and look up, and out, and all about,

And suddenly God is everywhere.

"How your goodness and kindness pursue me,
every day of my life."

Psalm 23

You will hardly believe your ear, Lord,

since, as you know, I like to divide my time equally

between feeling sorry for myself,

and asking you to make things better for me.

But just this once, I'd like to thank you

for all those things,

beginning with the gift of life itself,

that you have showered on me

for no earthly reason that I can see,

except that inexplicably,

in the face of selfishness and ingratitude

of monumental proportions and longevity,

you love me.

And beyond existence, bounty, beauty,

besides thought and sight and sound,

color, play, cold water, red wine and good food,

love and laughter, friends and home,

you gave us yourself in your son

and through him a promise that the one great catch

in your bounty—death—

was now revoked beyond the grave.

So forgive me, please,

the next time my insatiable self asks,

"What have you done for me lately?"

"Do not let my soul fall among the wicked,
or condemn me along with men of blood,
men guilty of great crimes,
whose hands are heavy with bribes.
For I live my life in innocence.
Redeem me for this, have mercy.
For my foot stays in the right path,
and I worship you."

Psalm 26

The psalmist sounds a trifle self-justifying and smug.

A bit like the parable of the publican and the sinner.

But perhaps he's got a point that I could make with God.

It's certainly true that I haven't done much that's virtuous.

But at least I can boast of not doing much that's evil.

Is God interested in such feeble claims?

I give you, Lord, the sins I could have sinned.

I hope they cancel out the ones I have committed.

God have pity on me,

for I am in your hands.

This illness consumes me,

brings out the worst in me,

makes me fearful and weak,

self-pitying and whining.

I know I should suffer with dignity,

take consolation in joining in your agony.

But when the pain comes my noble resolve disappears,

leaving me defenseless and alone.

Others see me and offer sympathetic looks,

and words well-meant but hollow.

How can they know?

Why me, Lord?

And worse, why not them?

I fear death more than pain.

Sometimes I think I can see it lurking close.

The doctor does his best, I'm sure.

But fails somehow to see the urgency:

This is *me!*

Yet can I pray for miracles?

Yes. If not of healing, then for faith.

Help me regain my hope and life in you.

Psalm 31

Happy are those whose faults are forgiven,
whose sins you have blotted out!"

Psalm 32

An act of perfect contrition is rendered imperfect

when one wonders whether it was perfect,

because if it isn't then sin remains,

and, remaining, threatens my salvation.

So I'm more worried about me than about offending God,

and that's imperfect.

That was the childhood riddle.

So off to the confessional to make sure.

Sweet relief in certain absolution.

Ninety-nine and ninety-nine-one-hundredths percent pure!

(For feeling so righteous, deduct the fraction.)

Thus were acres of sins cut down and hauled away.

But a thick stubble of guilt still lies

in the field of my unconscious,

which no amount of confessing seems to raze.

So, perfect or not, I most sincerely say:

I have sinned and I am sorry.

Forgiveness from God and man I pray.

*"The poor send up their cry, and God hears,
and helps them in their misery."*

Psalm 34

That cry is very loud these days.

Drought and famine,

war and oppression,

disease and starvation.

More than sparrows are falling to the ground.

Shall we reproach God for this indifference,

this wanton squandering of life?

No sooner born than dead (and sometimes sooner);

spaced out with a few months of misery.

Many men have turned away from God for just this.

Rather believe in nothing than a God

whose cruelest sport mocks life.

Or is it that God should reproach us?

That he hears through our ears,

and sees through our eyes.

And we are deaf and blind.

We did not create their plight, we say.

Don't be totally sure.

It is too vast a problem for anyone to solve, we explain.

For any *one*, quite true.

But for everyone?

Justice, God's justice for the poor!

It calls outside every door.

"Do not become obsessed with wickedness.
Don't envy those who do wrong and escape punishment.
For as frost kills the grass of summer
And burns brown the green fields
Their time of retribution will come."

Psalm 37

This is sound advice, ignored by many

who spend so much time resenting the success of others,

who, in their judgment, are chronic wrong-doers,

that they have little time to do much good themselves.

They complain loudly to their neighbors

and to God when their neighbors tune them out,

that this shameless lack of justice

is an affront to justice—human and divine.

Who knows if the wrongful will get theirs in the end.

They want to see them brought low now.

See how the righteous suffer

awaiting the vengeance of God.

"Lord, you have given me but a few years of life,
from a limitless supply you have on hand.
You treat me like a gust of wind
That leaves a ripple on the mirror lake
and then passes on without a trace.
You leave me with no security.
I could die tomorrow like the breeze.
I find it hard to count on anything."

Psalm 39

That's an age-old grievance lodged at least once

by nearly everyone who's ever lived.

It must stick in God's ear like a nettle.

When will they ever learn?

Those who came from nothing expect everything.

Have they thought, these ingrates, that it is
something of a luxury

even to be able to exist, never mind for how long?

A stone exists but does not complain.

Nor does it move or think or love.

They want to live forever—

Well, I've even given them that.

But just past their nose they cannot see

The boggling gift beyond—Eternity.

"As the thirsty doe seeks out the woodland stream,
so my soul aches for you, my God."

Psalm 42

Where is my faith of yesteryear?

Where the sense of presence,

bright and warm and real,

that radiated from the altars of my youth?

I could go and kneel and see and be

with you in a way that I can just recall today.

Now, when I pray the words fly away—

Where? I can no longer see you there.

Faith by reason is a cold, thin air

that's hard to breathe,

that brings no warmth to a frigid heart.

Perhaps I must learn to be a child again,

if that's what it takes to be let back in.

"Why so depressed my spirit,
why do you sigh so forlornly?
Put your hope in God.
For I shall see and praise him yet,
my savior and my God."

Psalm 43

In descending order we place our hope:

In knowledge,

in skill,

in luck,

in miracles,

and when all fails where can we turn?

To bleak despair?

And in the heart of darkness . . .

can it be?

A speck of light

that grows from nothing.

For when all is lost at last,

there remains only what was first:

Hope, our God, in thee.

"Now you have deserted and scorned us,
you no longer lead our armies into battle.
You permit the enemy to defeat us,
and attack us when and where they will."

Psalm 44

We sang "Glory, Glory Hallelujah . . ."

and you unleashed the lightning of your terrible swift sword.

We sang "Over There . . ."

and you came with us.

We praised you, Lord, while we passed the ammunition.

We came in on a wing and a prayer.

There were no atheists in our foxholes.

Our chaplains braved shot and shell.

In God we trusted, might making right.

And we won and won and won.

But these last few times out . . .

Where have you been?

The other side doesn't even believe in you!

You must know that.

They're just gooks of some description—heathen scum.

To whom life is notoriously cheap.

Not that we accuse you of being on their side.

But why are you no longer on ours?

Are you trying to tell us something?

"Do not envy the person who stores up riches,
whose fame and fortune grows huge.
For soon enough death will call him down
to where neither wealth nor glory can follow."

Psalm 49

"You Can't Take It with You"—that's for sure.

And the dark implication in that word "down"?

Must that be the destination of all the rich?

Jesus said it will be harder for them to

enter the kingdom than for a camel to pass

through the eye of a needle.

There will be wealth and vainglory

in neither heaven nor hell.

But there would seem to be grave danger

for those who acquire them on earth.

I certainly haven't done so,

But it's not for lack of trying.

I wonder if lusting after fame and riches,

even unsuccessfully,

carries the same dire consequences?

If so, a lot of us who feel justified

may in fact be in big trouble.

*"Create a clean heart in me, O God,
and renew a right spirit within me."*

Psalm 51

The Psalmist's heart was heavy with the guilt of a great sin.

I have committed no murder.

Nor betrayed anyone to death or prison.

I haven't (fashionable as it is) slept with my neighbor's wife.

But add my name to his petition,

for my heart is calloused over with layers of smaller sins:

Of indifference, spite, lassitude;

of self-indulgence, malice and creeping cynicism.

So imperviously armored it takes a sword thrust

(or a bomb)

to reach an awareness of you, Lord,

that once came constantly to mind.

You come down to the earth and water it;

in it you have hidden vast riches;

Your rivers flow to the brim,

with water for our crops.

You drench our furrows with rain,

You soften the heart with sweet showers.

You crown the year with a fruitful bounty.

You leave abundance in your footsteps.

You make the desert bloom

and decorate it with burgeoning flocks.

You wrap our hillsides in sweetness

and clothe our valleys with golden wheat.

What rejoicing! What singing!

Psalm 65

"Lord, now that I am old and gray,
do not desert me.
Let me live to tell the younger generation
of your goodness, strength and power."

Psalm 71

Old age began the day I first saw death.

Not just dying, but the certainty of my own death.

And, having seen it, I can never forget

that you have numbered my days.

And then I think sorrowful thoughts

of all that might have been,

of all the ways in which I've failed,

of all the losses, sadness, pain.

And worst, that no one seems to care,

that I won't be here for them to share.

Birthday cards from heartless children

are but crumbs before my appetite for gratitude.

Ingrates! I gave them everything.

Life itself—learning, laughter, home and love.

But wait!

With age at least and last should come understanding.

Could it just possibly be

that you might make the same complaints of me?

Remember that God stands invisible.

in the midst of every human assembly,

above the shoulder of everybody who holds power in
their hands.

"Do not, through you, let justice be mocked," he cries.

"Do not favor the wicked at the expense of the orphan and
the widow.

Be fair to the miserable and destitute.

Use your power to uplift the weak and needy,

rescue them from the jaws of the corrupt.

With this I charge you in my name!"

Psalm 82

"What is God saying? I am listening.
God's words hold the key to peace
—for his people, for all who are his friends.
We must renounce this folly.
For those who will hear him, his saving help is at hand
And peace will reign in all the world."

Psalm 85

We who live in the incipient eye of the holocaust

should take these words to heart.

But heeding them how do we convince others
to do the same?

We are people of peace, we protest,

but can we turn our backs, much less our cheeks,

upon those who insist on keeping their weapons
at the ready

simply because we peaceful realists also keep ours?

Step back a pace, we say, and we will do the same.

So would we, they reply, but please,

to show your sincerity, you go first.

And so it goes, the endless standoff.

God's words of peace fall fruitless to the ground.

His patience is said to extend into blank infinity.

And at this rate that is where we may
next hear him speak.

"Let me wake to a morning filled with your love.
Let me rejoice and be happy.
Let me see how much you can do for me.
Let your bounty be upon me.
Make all I do succeed."

Psalm 90

That's baldly put, I must admit.

What they call a "give me" prayer.

It is also childish and out of fashion,

reducing God to a sugar daddy.

Yet, there it is, in the Book.

And who am I to try to be nobler.

Selfishness is to be overcome.

But selfish I am.

So, while it may be the least of prayers,

at least it's honest.

If you dwell in the house of God,

live your lives in the shadow of his love,

you can call upon him for everything.

You can say to him: "You are my refuge,

my bastion, my God in whom I place all trust."

There no disaster can overtake you,

no evil come upon you while you sleep.

He will put you in the charge of his angels

to guard you wheresoever you may go.

For he has said:

"I will rescue all who cling to me.

I shield all who know my name.

I abide with them in times of trouble.

I bring them sustenance and safety.

I grant them a life long and full

and show them that in me they are saved."

Psalm 91

Humankind endures no longer than a blade of grass,

no longer than a wild flower do we last.

One puff of wind and we are gone,

never to be seen again.

But God's love for those who love him

prevails for all eternity.

As does his goodness to our children's children

so long as they keep faith in him

and his will perform.

What would we be without God's love?

Where would we be?

Let us praise God now with fervor in our hearts,

now and evermore.

Psalm 103

From the depths of my being I call to God.

Lord, heed my cry!

Listen with compassion to my plea.

If you refused to forgive us our sins,

who, Lord, would manage to survive?

But you do grant us your forgiveness

and we bless you for your mercy.

I wait for your forgiveness, my heart longs for it.

I trust in your covenant,

my heart counts on you, Lord,

more than the sentry, the rising of the sun.

For mercy and redemption,

the salving of my pain,

can come only from God's goodness,

which falls like cleansing rain.

Psalm 130

Lord, I harbor no great ambitions,

I do not cast high my sights.

I am not one for great affairs

or for grasping things beyond my reach.

Sufficient for me is peace of mind,

the quiet tranquility of a child

well content in its mother's arms.

But such trust and peace

I know full well

can come only from you,

in whose sustaining love we bask.

Please keep me there is all I ask.

Psalm 131

"To you, Lord, I turn my eyes.
Shelter me, do not leave me vulnerable.
Keep me clear of the traps that evil sets."

Psalm 141

My first temptation was to steal.

To take, really, a red wagon from a store.

I did it, feckless child, in a brash rush.

Collared instantly by a mortified mother

who shuddered at the little criminal

emerging suddenly from her pride and joy.

And the shame I didn't know,

grew instantly from the hurt in her eyes.

I never stole again.

But there were heated years to follow,

when temptations were of the flesh.

So strong they blocked all others,

making them unrecognizable in the smoke.

All the smaller failings lurked,

looking harmless and benign,

but well inside my defenses now,

entrenched and camouflaged.

A lesson to be learned from the cliche:

You can win the battle and lose the war.

The chaste liar's lie stinks as badly as the wanton's.

The faithful cheat will steal all but love.

PART THREE

Prayers and Meditations on the Rosary

"In the actual, living, human person who is the Virgin Mother of Christ are all the poverty and all the wisdom of all the saints. It all came to them through her, and is in her. The sanctity of all the saints is a participation in her sanctity, because in the order He has established God wills that all graces come to men through Mary."

Thomas Merton

"Let us mull over the words of the Gospel in frequent meditation, let us ever keep in mind the example of Mary, the blessed Mother of God, so that we also may be found humble in the sight of God, that being subject in due honor also to our neighbor, we may deserve together with her to be exalted forever."

St. Bede the Venerable

"The steadfast faith of Our Lady shines forth in the Gospels. For almost all the other followers of Our Lord either fled him at one time or another, or doubted his resurrection after death, except his dear mother; in commemoration thereof the Church in its yearly Tenebrae service leaves her candle burning still when all those which signify the apostles and disciples, are one by one put out."

St. Thomas More

THE JOYFUL MYSTERIES OF THE ROSARY

Opening Meditation

IT is especially fitting that we begin the Rosary with the Joyful Mysteries. The Rosary is a meditation on the central events in the life of Jesus as given us in the Gospels. The Joyful Mysteries celebrate key moments from the first two chapters of the evangelist Luke—the Infancy Narratives. So we rightly open our hearts to the beginning of Christ's life on earth—to the instant of his conception by the power of God and the dawn of our hope and joy in the great Good News that the angel brought to us all.

The joy that animates these five mysteries is not the passing, raucous exuberance of the moment—not the gaiety of a party or a victory celebration. It is a far quieter, greater, emotion that is involved here—a joy that is born deep in the soul and which will endure the test of bad times as well as good. And that is something very much worth bearing in mind as we strive to bring these Joyful Mysteries alive in our twentieth century hearts. The deep Christian joy of these mysteries sustains us even in moments of trial and pain, in fact it is their light which illuminates and redeems these hours, making them bearable.

The center of a mystery is by definition hidden, but the closer we can come to this center the more powerfully can we feel its transforming force. There is something in that hidden heart of mystery which works a great wonder. Sorrow, doubt, fear, suffering, bafflement, are somehow turned around and, if not destroyed, are seen as mere blurs and specks against the larger, abiding joy of the promise of salvation and life eternal.

The First Joyful Mystery

THE ANNUNCIATION

THE story of the life of Jesus begins with the words of the angel to Mary, with the words which we repeat over and over as we pray the Rosary: "Hail Mary, full of grace . . ." The Word was made flesh in the instant of Mary's response: "Behold, I am the handmaid of the Lord; let it be done to me according to your word."

Mary accepts her vocation with these words even though the evangelist tells us that she was troubled and perplexed in the awesome instant. Like us, she did not know what the future held in store, but in spite of this she would accept God's will as her own.

Acceptance of this order is not blind resignation to fate, rather it is an active embracing of God's will and plan for our lives, an implicit agreement to take up the challenge and make the most of our role, however humble or exalted that may prove to be.

Mary transformed her troubles, doubts and fears with her *fiat*. We can do the same by prayerfully and actively accepting our vocation, our call to life, each day.

The Second Joyful Mystery

THE VISITATION

WHOLE books have been written on the underlying meanings and symbolism of Mary's visit to her pregnant relative, Elizabeth. But on the simplest of human levels it must have been both thrilling and again somewhat frightening to receive from Elizabeth the first confirmation by another human being of the wonder that had overtaken her.

The child in Elizabeth's womb "leapt" in recognition of the Godchild carried in Mary's. But this is not why Mary went to Elizabeth. Rather she undertook what in those days would have been an arduous four-day journey simply to be of comfort and service to her cousin. It was an act of love and, quite literally, she brought Christ with her on her journey.

In meditating on this delightful incident, and hearing the words of the Magnificat afresh, let us pray that we can keep this spirit of charity alive in ourselves when we take up the challenge to bring the Christ that is in us to others so that they may respond with the joy of Elizabeth and the child in her womb.

The Third Joyful Mystery

THE NATIVITY

ASK any good parents and they will tell you that the birth of their firstborn child stands out as one of the most joyful moments of their lives. And any mother has a special insight into the nature of this mystery of childbirth—the pain of labor that is displaced with an all-pervading, enduring sense of joy.

In the figure of the helpless, newborn savior we all share in this mystery of joy. It is his birth and our own which we celebrate—our birth to the promise of eternal life from the labor of pain that sin and daily existence can impose. Who more helpless and less threatening than a baby—but who more filled with fresh promise for the fulfillment of impossible dreams?

At the moment of his birth, Christ identified himself most fully with the helplessness and weakness of the humanity he shares completely with us. He does not come with trumpets on a fiery cloud of omnipotence and judgment but as an infant calling for our acceptance and love.

Let us pray that this ultimate act of identification and humility on the part of God will keep us open and humble before those whom we would teach, lead and love.

The Fourth Joyful Mystery

THE PRESENTATION OF JESUS IN THE TEMPLE

THE presence of the Holy Spirit is made tangible in this rich mystery which shows again how joy overrides and transforms sorrow. Old Testament meets New when the Spirit moves the ancient Simeon to recognize the long awaited Messiah in the presence of the forty-day-old infant which Mary, according to custom, offers to the service of God.

Simeon is moved to tears of joy even as he realizes that this recognition and his final prophecy to Mary signal the end of his own life—for the Spirit had promised him he would be kept alive long enough to see the Lord. His frightening message to Mary that her heart would be pierced by the swords of sorrow could only affirm more fully her growing joy in yet another public confirmation that she held salvation in her arms.

The presentation may be seen as a formal dedication of Christ's mission—a public pledge and offering. Let it become for us a model of our own need to offer ourselves each day to God.

The Fifth Joyful Mystery

THE FINDING OF JESUS IN THE TEMPLE

IT is easy to associate ourselves with the joy of parents who have found a lost child after searching for nearly three days. Once again, great joy emerges transformed from the keenest of anxieties. But there should be joy, too, in hearing the first words which Jesus himself speaks to us in the Gospels. He tells Mary and Joseph—and we cannot help but feel that he spoke with a certain youthful brashness—that they should not have concerned themselves since it is time he was about his Father's business.

A less familiar, but more fitting translation of his words reads, "Where else would you expect to find me but in my Father's house?" To Jesus, it was the natural place to be and we can rejoice in this statement of the young Messiah's self-realization of his mission. It was also the first demonstration of his power, purpose and knowledge in confounding the scribes with a wisdom beyond his years.

But let us reflect, too, from the point of view of Mary and Joseph, and remind ourselves that we must look for the light of Christ in the most unexpected places in our lives, and that we must keep looking even when we do not find him at once.

THE SORROWFUL MYSTERIES OF THE ROSARY

Opening Meditation

A mystery is something we cannot understand or fully explain. There are mysteries of faith which science will never be able to account for and which tradition teaches will be answered only in the life to come. Belief in Christ's promise of redemption and everlasting life is, in itself, a mystery. We believe but we wonder: Why? How? What will it be like? That promise is a happy, a glorious mystery.

But leading up to its proclamation by Jesus were a series of searing, painful, even terrible experiences which he had to pass through—much as we are all called upon to pass through bitter suffering, sadness and death in order to come to the moment when we can claim the glorious promise of everlasting life with him.

These trials, these experiences of suffering which Jesus chose to pass through rather than avoid, we call the Sorrowful Mysteries—the Agony in the Garden, the Scourging and abuse of the Roman soldiers at the pillar, the Crowning with Thorns, the Carrying of the Cross, and finally, his Crucifixion and Death on the Cross.

As we well know, there is nothing mysterious about pain itself. But there is plenty to wonder at in the *why* of Christ's suffering and the manner of his death. As with any true mystery, we will not arrive at the total answer by reasoning or scientific experiment. But that does not prevent us from searching for as much meaning and understanding as we can find in these unhappy moments when our God chose to suffer in the same way that we do.

To wonder at these mysteries is to experience sorrow—sorrow for Jesus and sorrow for ourselves and our loved ones, sorrow for Mary, the mother of Jesus and all his disciples and friends who witnessed his suffering. So let us wonder and feel again the anguish of those dreadful but somehow necessary hours when Jesus felt the weight of all humanity and all the sufferings of tender, mortal flesh, all the mocking, the taunts and indignities which humankind still continues to inflict upon each other.

Let us pray that by entering into these sorrowful moments we may become part of the ultimately glorious mystery of salvation.

The First Sorrowful Mystery

THE AGONY IN THE GARDEN

THESE hours were among the worst that Jesus suffered, for the pain inflicted came from within. Mental anguish can be as great as physical torture. This was the moment when the awful confrontation presented itself to Jesus. He must freely embrace the ordeal ahead of him. There was still time to flee, to change, to soften the events ahead. Why should all this fall on him? Why must the Father's will be worked out in such grisly fashion? Would even this pageant of suffering serve to convince and convert the indifferent world? Even his most intimate and trusted followers were so unaware, so uncaring that they fell asleep. Couldn't this bitter cup be taken from his lips? And yet all the while he knew the answer was no—and that he himself would drain the cup completely for the sake of the kingdom whose gates he would open for us all.

The Second Sorrowful Mystery

THE SCOURGING AT THE PILLAR

IT could have been but small consolation to a man being lashed with studded flails that the one who ordered the scourging was thereby trying to save his life. This was Jesus' first encounter with physical pain—the first taste from the cup he had agreed to drink in the Garden of Olives. Be assured that the pain he felt was as real to him as to any other human—perhaps made even worse by the knowledge that Pilate's attempt to earn the sympathy of the mob was doomed to fail. Being brutalized is something we all fear, Jesus experienced the profound sorrow of being a victim.

Let us all try to share it with him.

The Third Sorrowful Mystery

THE CROWNING WITH THORNS

IT'S possible that after the agony of the flogging, the sting of the thorns, pressed into his scalp, seemed almost minor to Jesus. The real suffering here came from being mocked and ridiculed. The soldiers threw a ragged purple cloak over his lacerated back, gave him a crown of thorns and a reed for a scepter and taunted him as the most pathetic and powerless man ever to pretend to royalty.

Think how we all react to even the smallest implication that we are ridiculous. Pride is the tender spot, the most vulnerable. Think how it must have flayed the spirit of the Son of God to be mocked by those for whom he was about to give up his life.

The Fourth Sorrowful Mystery

THE CARRYING OF THE CROSS

THE humiliation was well-calculated. The condemned not only had to bear the weight of the instrument of his suffering and death, but he had to march a gauntlet of jeering, leering, curious people—entertainment for bored city dwellers. The cross was staggeringly heavy; it cut down into an already lacerated back and pressed the cap of thorns into the side of his head. Jesus fell repeatedly. The soldiers made Simon carry the cross part of the way, not out of compassion but because they feared the victim might cheat them of the crucifixion by dying along the way.

When we feel that our load of pain or humiliation is too heavy to bear—even for a single instant—let us go back to the way of the Cross and take another step with Jesus.

The Fifth Sorrowful Mystery

THE CRUCIFIXION

IT all culminates here—the end and the beginning. A whirlpool of suffering draws Jesus down from tormented consciousness to death. The hammers, the nails, the thirst—an agony of hours climaxed by the thrust of a spear. The humiliation of being posted as an example of the rewards of crime and infamy when totally innocent, the torture of seeing this suffering reflected in your mother's eyes . . . the necessity to once more quell the refrain from the Garden: is it possible that all of this is for nothing?

There is only pain now and faith in the Father to sustain the promise of a resurrection. Then blackness. At the instant of his death the only hope left had to reside in the faith of his mother and the scattered disciples. Let us ponder these things and strive to count ourselves forever among their number.

THE GLORIOUS MYSTERIES OF THE ROSARY

Opening Meditation

IN the traditional sequence for saying the three decades of the Rosary, the Glorious Mysteries come last. And, you will recall, there is an obvious reason for this. The opening Joyful Mysteries are concerned with the infancy and youth of Jesus' life. The Sorrowful Mysteries center on the events of his passion and death. And the Glorious call for our prayerful reflection on the mysteries which followed the death of Jesus on the cross—the Resurrection, his Ascension into Heaven, the Descent of the Holy Spirit on Pentecost, the Assumption of Mary the Virgin Mother, and, finally, her Crowning in Heaven.

Glorious is a word that we don't hear too often these days, so it might be well to refresh our memories. We know what emotions are summed up by the words joyful and sorrowful—but glorious is precisely what? The dictionary is of some help here. Glory is defined as praise, honor or distinction extended by a common consent, and, further, as the splendor and beatific happiness of heaven. Synonyms for glorious are listed as resplendent, delightful and wonderful.

And it is these last two words that I would like to focus on as we recite together the Glorious Mysteries—let us search out the delight, the wonder, the *wonderfulness* which lie at the heart of these splendid moments. Rejoice, revel even, in their implications for yourself, for us all.

For we, through the boundless and unwarranted generos-

ity and extravagant, preposterous outpouring of love that is
God himself—we, unimaginable as it seems, do share, par-
ticipate in the glorious mystery of Christ's rising from the
dead, his ascension unto life everlasting, the coming of the
Holy Spirit, Mary's assumption and crowning in heaven.

The First Glorious Mystery

THE RESURRECTION

HE is risen. He is not here!

Surely those must be the most glorious words ever spoken to humankind. So portentous were they that they were given in charge of an angel to deliver. In their simplicity lies a wonder beyond our comprehension, a hope beyond our wildest dreams, a gift beyond anything we can deserve. For in this most central of all Christian mysteries is the promise of victory over death, of the power of goodness over evil, and of nothing short of eternal life.

Had not Christ been born, the words could not have been spoken. Had not Christ died they would not have been possible. But had he not risen all would have been in vain.

But he did rise—gloriously—and in his resurrection we all share because God, in his infinite goodness, first shared his divine life with us in the person of his only son.

Let us rejoice at this greatest piece of good news ever given.

The Second Glorious Mystery

THE ASCENSION

THE disciples must have had some mixed feelings about the Ascension. Awe, certainly, at still another marvelous proof of the divinity of Jesus. But fear, too, and perhaps sorrow. For the Lord was no longer with them.

But the Ascension can be seen as inevitable, as the only possible closing for the great drama of salvation which had been played out before their eyes. It was the final moment of the forty days of glory which they had shared with the risen Christ.

The Ascension is perhaps the most graphic of all the mysteries. What believer has not tried to picture the scene for him or herself. Many great artists have given us their vision of the moment.

However your imagination portrays it, the important thing for us now is to wonder and rejoice in the event, to let our spirits rise with Jesus—to reflect on the Ascension when we feel deserted or despondent. For who, recalling that moment of power and grandeur, can feel cut off from the love of God, our Father in Heaven?

The Third Glorious Mystery

THE DESCENT OF THE HOLY SPIRIT

AS we noted before, the Disciples may have felt a sense of loss when Our Lord ascended into heaven. He had left them with a promise that someone would come to take his place and abide with them. Yet how could they know what a gift and what a presence would be sent to them—invisible, to be sure, but a force, a spirit which would fill them in a more complete and intimate way than even the sight and sound of Jesus had? The spirit of God came over them and was in them and sustained and animated them.

Again we are in the presence of an awesome mystery, but rejoicing, wonder, delight are much more called for than fear. All of these mysteries are bringing news that seems simply too good to be true. Why should God do so much for us—for us who have done so little for him? It seems that simple acceptance is all he asks in return—acceptance and love.

And love is the spirit which he sent to us all on Pentecost. Love that is strong, vibrant, filled with the unfathomable spirit of God. And that love, that spirit dwells in each of us today as strongly as it did in the disciples who gathered in that wonder-filled room. We have only to open ourselves, accept, delight and share that Holy Spirit with those around us through care, service, and most of all, through love.

The Fourth Glorious Mystery

THE ASSUMPTION OF MARY

WHEN the poet Wordsworth referred to Mary as "Our tainted nature's solitary boast," he was referring, of course, to her Immaculate Conception, to her unique freedom from the effects of original sin. One of those effects was death. And so, by strong and ancient tradition of the Church, and now by dogma as well we believe Mary did not die the death that comes to all others but was assumed bodily into heaven—the mystery to which we devote this decade of prayers of honor and intercession.

And in her bodily assumption we can find pre-figured our own spiritual assumption into heaven—into union with the Father and the Son and the Holy Spirit. For, while free of the taint of original sin, Mary was fully human and in celebrating her certain attainment of heaven we are given demonstration that the gates of heaven—through the mystery of the resurrection—are now open indeed to the likes of us.

The Fifth Glorious Mystery

THE CROWNING OF MARY

MARY, whose heart was pierced by the sword of seven sorrows, who wept as she saw her son struggling with a heavy cross while crowned with a cruel circle of thorns—Mary is now given a glorious crown in heaven.

The beautiful and ancient tradition of the coronation of Mary in heaven celebrates not only the great beauty and dignity of her life, but her pre-eminent role as the mother of Jesus. It is her humanity incarnated in his person which was the flesh which he shares with all of us—so that we in turn can share in his eternal life.

The coronation of Mary also symbolizes her status as mediatrix of the grace which flows from God to us by virtue of the redeeming role of her Son. The Blessed Virgin becomes the mother of us all, a queenly mother, but a gentle, compassionate mother to the flawed humans of all the passing centuries till the end of time. Her crowning is a gloriously appropriate way in which to end these meditations on the mysteries of the rosary which is dedicated to her name.

"Grant, we beseech you, O Lord, that meditating on the mysteries of the rosary of the Blessed Virgin Mary, we may imitate what they contain and obtain what they promise."

PART FOUR

Reflections

REFLECTIONS ON THE FEAST
OF THE IMMACULATE CONCEPTION

MOST children, when they are old enough to think about it at all, tend to regard their parents—especially their mothers —as absolutely perfect (and perhaps all-powerful, as well). It's a natural enough reaction and one that is often consciously or unconsciously promoted by parents. A mother whom friends and husband may know from experience to be possessed of a quick temper and habitual impatience may make a positively heroic and successful display of long-suffering calm and infinite tolerance toward her small children. But as we advance we begin to see the flaws, not only in our parents, but in virtually everyone. It is part of the growing pattern and the unfortunate but necessary process of disillusionment that leads to maturity. So much so that by the time we are young adults most of us are made uneasy by the rare encounter with someone who seems genuinely to be perfect, to generate an aura not only of goodness but who seems possessed of no faults whatsoever. Such people should inspire nothing but love and emulation on our part. Too often we react to them with naked resentment and a prying suspicion aimed at unmasking them in order to get at the hypocrite we are sure lurks out of sight just beneath the surface.

Today, contrary to the gospel passage from Luke, we celebrate not the Annunciation (the conception of Jesus through the power of God's Spirit); neither do we celebrate the Virgin Birth. We are, in fact, commemorating the perfection of Mary—her freedom from all sin, even that of primal, original sin. So, as Wordsworth wrote, we are confronted with a unique person—"Our tainted nature's solitary boast." If Mary were here with us now, would we regard her with the reverence, awe and piety which centuries of Catholic worship and devotion have built up around her? Or would we, if we knew her simply as one of our poverty-stricken fellow parishioners, resent her for being so perfect, so long-suffering, so noble and selfless in the face of her adversity and low station among us?

She must be putting up a false front, we might think. Her case is hopeless, her expectations nil, so she tries to impress us with her ceaseless piety and charity. She's too good to be true because she's got nothing to lose and it's a good bet she takes it out on her husband and child. Spare us from having to live with a paragon like that.

This human tendency to resent, or at least to be put off by unmitigated human perfection is reflected in the slightly irreverent but nonetheless revealing joke about Jesus and the woman taken in adultery. The angry crowd was threatening her when Jesus ordered: "Let you who is without sin among you cast the first stone." And immediately a small pebble comes sailing out of the crowd and hits the woman lightly on the shoulder. "Mother!" Jesus cries in exasperation.

The fact that since Mary no other human being, including the saints, can make that claim of sinless perfection should not stop us—as it did not stop the saints—from recognizing it as an ideal toward which we should strive. Mary, about whom we really know so little, is nonetheless a model not just for mothers and women, but for fathers and men, as well. Well, it was easy for her, we can say, after all, if she was conceived without sin how could she go wrong? But hypothetically Mary was not any freer from distractions and temptations than any of us. Even Jesus was not spared a thoroughly rigorous round of temptations by Satan, in person. And Mary certainly had more than her share of poverty, disappointments, frustrations and bitter sorrow.

Coming back down to earth in the late 20th century, let us recognize that we are a long way from the historical Mary and Jesus, a long way from the childlike credulity of many of our early Christian forerunners who did not have our latter-day expertise in biblical exegesis and skepticism about the literalness of every word of scripture. It's very difficult to demonstrate Marian perfection and Christian love in the middle of a morning rush hour or in an office where everything and everyone seems to conspire against us. It's difficult for a modern mother, who may well be working at a job or profession as well, to radiate the calm and patient forbearance of Mary, the model mother of us all. Our sins may not be original but they are—measured against such a seemingly exalted standard as Mary—legion. Let's face it, the story of Mary the perfect human being is a lovely idea and a nice story to tell the kids, but it's got nothing to do with us.

Does not the real meaning of the doctrine of the Immaculate Conception lie somewhere in between the two extremes we have outlined—the hopeless but praiseworthy effort to emulate Mary and seek human perfection or writing off this vision of her as some sort of supergood person totally irrelevant to our lives? The proclamation of the dogma of the Immaculate Conception of Mary—that she was spared the stain and effects of original sin (one of which was death which then postulated the necessity of the dogma of Mary's Assumption into heaven) troubled a number of Catholics when it was issued in the mid-nineteenth century.

England's brilliant Cardinal John Henry Newman, for one, thought that it was unnecessary—not because it was wrong, but because Mary's role and goodness were so self-evident in the gospels that no delimiting formal human proclamation need be made. He had a point, because formalizing something tends to make people think about it in just one way— the way the formalizers were thinking at a particular moment in history. Today it is perhaps more relevant to us that Mary embodied as much human goodness as a person could embody rather than that she was absolutely perfect and free from original sin. We can learn to emulate this sort of goodness if it is embodied in a model with whom we can identify —a person of warmth, compassion, forgiveness, and, above all, a person who is good not just for the sake of goodness but because it is the *greatest* good to love others even when they fail us and each other.

PRACTICAL APPLICATION

Instead of being suspicious, skeptical, turned off and even affronted by the good that we encounter in people—even in people whom we know to be less than perfect most of the time, let us learn to aprpeciate it, respond to it, reflect it, nurture it in both the other person and in ourselves. There's all too little goodness going around these days. Let us savor it and nourish it where and when we can so that, like a newly planted seed that lies open to the not-so-tender mercies of nature, it may grow and thrive and multiply among us.

REFLECTIONS ON CHRISTMAS GIFTS

SCORES of variations have been celebrated in art, words and song, but the traditional scene contains these elements: a warm and spacious room dominated by a lavishly decorated evergreen tree which reaches to the ceiling and is topped by an angel or a star; to offset the cold and falling snow outside, a crackling fire under a mantel festooned with greenery banked dangerously close to the guttering candles of the Yule log; an awe-inspiring pile of lavishly wrapped presents in boxes of tantalizing sizes and shapes; a cut-glass punch-bowl brimming with creamy eggnog on a table overflowing with food; and most important of all—the room is packed with people you love, old and young. And then the present-opening ritual begins, a splendid chaos of appreciative cries, ripping paper and flying ribbon.

Contrasted with the austerity of the cave and manger there seems very little resemblance between our scene and the first Christmas, very little in such opulence and materialism that emulates the poverty endorsed by the Gospels. Indeed, unless our scene includes a creche or some Christmas carols playing on the stereo, it is unlikely that many or any of the people opening presents will give more than a passing thought to the one in whose name they are gathered. Yet to many more Christians than attend midnight Mass, this scene is the essence of Christmas, what they travel impossible miles to become a part of, what they miss and mourn if they cannot join in, what they cherish in nostaligic reveries about "Christmas Past." Is there, then, something greedy and hypocritical about the traditional way most of us celebrate and imagine Christmas? Is Christ pushed out of the heart of his so-called followers at the very instant when they should be celebrating the central mystery of their faith—the Incarnation, the flesh-taking of God?

Many sermons in the past have been devoted to answering that question in the affirmative, to condemning the creeping materialism that each year seems to mount its sales campaign a little earlier and pushes the image of cave and manger further into the shadows. There have been countless campaigns launched by concerned religious leaders "to keep Christ in Christmas"; hundreds of books, pamphlets and Catholic press editorials have urged us to make our family celebrations of Christmas more spiritual; generations of parochial school children have been admonished to set their hearts and minds more on the Babe in the crib than on that new bike. But, in good times and bad, there are still presents under the tree, still expectant little fingers probing tissue paper, still exhausted, financially overextended parents playing Santa Claus in the small hours of Christmas morning. And no amount of preaching, no amount of condemnation is going to stop them.

Nor should it, because the giving and receiving of presents is not only a legitimate Christmas tradition but it is as central to the feast as the images in the creche—more so, really, since plaster figures can only remind us of a moment in history (a great moment to be sure) whereas the exchange of presents, rightly understood and exercised, is an active exercise of the love that was brought to earth in the Incarnation. In the Gospel for the Vigil of Christmas, Matthew says of the events surrounding the Annunciation that "all this took place to fulfill the words spoken by the Lord through the prophet: 'the virgin will conceive and give birth to a son and they will call him Emmanuel,' a name which means 'God-is-with-us.' " And the way the Lord is with us this Christmas, nearly 2,000 years after the first, is not in plaster images or carols, but in the reciprocal love we manifest to each other and to the world—the celebration of shared presence through shared presents. The Magi brought gifts to the infant Jesus to signal the importance of the overwhelming union of the divine with the human—certainly the most valuable gift ever given, and in comparison with which mere gold and spices could only be a token. Gifts exchanged in the true spirit of Christmas not only mirror this exchange but reincarnate that gift of love by recognizing our kinship with Jesus and with each other as daughters and sons of God.

It's not to collect three new ties and a bottle of after-shave lotion that a son braves the crowded skies between Los Angeles and Detroit to be with his parents and brothers and sisters at Christmas. It's not the gold in the brooch her childr n give her that lights up the eyes of the grandmother. It's not just the fact that the fur coat a husband gives his wife is indeed quite valuable and beautiful. And it's not even that it's the thought that counts. The thought certainly does count but there's more than a thought involved in the son's long, expensive and tiring journey; more than just an effort to say "thank you" to the grandmother; more than deep gratification in the mind of the husband who gives his wife a coat she thought she would never possess. Certainly materialism can blur and dim the true meaning of Christmas and there are many who exploit the spirit of the season for their own profit, but when we gather together to exchange gifts the real value resides not in the gifts, or even in the thoughtfulness and perhaps sacrifice that went into buying some of them. The real value is in the gathering itself, the celebration of what is lovable and priceless in each other, the sharing of self, the giving of self, the living affirmation of the great gift of Emmanuel, the God-who-is-with-us now, this Christmas day.

PRACTICAL APPLICATION

Perhaps a fitting "Christmas resolution" would be to extend this sharing of the gift of self to one another beyond the ritual of exchanging gifts. The period after Christmas is often one of let-down, bred partially from exhaustion, but also from a sense of frustration that everything didn't go as well as we had hoped, that we have missed out on something, of failure to convey all that was in our hearts through our gifts. With some effort and reflection on the mystery of incarnational love and its manifestation through human love we can try to be more generous with our expressions of it in words and through thoughtfulness. Let us, in fact, be spendthrifts who give the best and most valued Christmas gifts with free abandon to those we love all year long.

REFLECTIONS ON THE NEW YEAR

THE French have a word for it—or rather two words: "deja vu". Literally it means "already seen". *Webster's* defines it as "something overly or unpleasantly familiar." Deja vu afflicts us all at one time or another: the wife and mother who grits her teeth as she prepares her thousandth meal of the year; the commuter who sighs as he endures yet another wait for the bus that will take him on yet another jerky, drawn-out journey to work; the high-school teacher who looks out at yet another batch of freshman faces; and yes, the priest who struggles to come up with something fresh and challenging to tell a New Year's Day congregation. There is a cyclical nature to life, work and routine which is discouraging, sometimes depressing, even when we are in the best of health, free of major problems, and should be in the best of spirits.

Many are especially prone to deja vu at this time of the year. "Out with the old, in with the new," is a refrain we've not only heard too often, but one which, we know from long experience, to be a catch phrase that somehow never has taken hold in our lives. Looking down the long slope of the year from winter's dark perspective it is terribly difficult to see the spring, to experience the surge of new life, new energy, new zest for living that brings animation to our spirit. The Christmas and New Year's celebrations are behind us; slush and snow (even in a figurative sense), work and dull routine, long days and endless nights, stand between us and vacation. As the song says, "it seems I've stood and talked like this before." In a very real sense, if we're honest, part of us would be willing to throw away the calendar for the next three months, go into a trance or hibernate—

anything to escape that "overly and unpleasantly familiar" routine.

And that is tragic when you think about it. It's like saying we're willing to give up three months of our lives every year. And it doesn't have to be this way at all. If what is depressing us to this extent is in our heads, then let's turn our heads around. One way to do this is to transcend a bit from the routine that so absorbs us, to lift up our minds and our hearts to appreciate the good fortune that is ours, the great gifts of life and health that are ours too. And the even greater gifts that God has given us in his Son and in the promise of everlasting life which the Son brought to us. Today's first reading assures us that God lets his face shine upon us and grants us the abiding peace of this enduring life. Pauls tells us that we are not really slaves to the routine of work but with the Incarnation, through the accepting vessel of Mary, Mother of God, whose feast we celebrate today, we have become sons and daughters of God—brothers and sisters of Jesus himself.

Perhaps that's precisely what these seemingly dark days of winter are for, what our depression at starting over yet another time is meant to underline. If we resist the depression, cast off the dull preoccupation with the ordinary we can find a moment, a space in our lives to appreciate the great Christian reality of peace, blessedness, and the promise of eternal life. How can we be depressed or even think about throwing months out of the lives of such fortunate creatures as ourselves? As if to underscore this Luke tells of the wonders of the first days following the birth of Jesus, and the excitement of the shepherds (whose work surely qualifies as being deadly dull; in fact, when you think about it, what happens when you devote yourself completely to counting sheep?) The experience they had was extraordinary. "Everyone was astounded at what the shepherds had to say," writes Luke in massive understatement. Isn't it just as exciting still —if only one stops to think about it? If only one gets back to the magic of that moment when salvation, the greatest free gift of all time, came to earth heralded by wondrous signs and words. It was truly a close encounter of the divine sort, but this time the UFO identified itself as pure gift and love.

And how should we react? Luke tells us that as well: like Mary who "treasured all these things in her heart." We should find the time, especially at this season of the year, to unpack these same treasures from our hearts and hold them up to revel in the light that they give to these darkest days of the year, these darkest moments of our depression. Properly reappreciated they have the power to sweep away the cobwebs of deja vu and send us singing through the days and months ahead—not necessarily out loud, but as quietly joyful and at peace as was Mary, the Mother of God, on the day when she bore her son—*the* Son—off to the temple to receive the name by which we are all saved and through which we shall live forever.

PRACTICAL APPLICATION

The next time you feel tempted to drown yourself in the resignation and depression of deja vu, to wish that you could just go to sleep and wake up in three or four months with all the dreary routine of winter behind you, stop and count those great Christian blessings just enumerated. Life under such blessings is a celebration and people at celebrations don't go around sighing and moaning with boredom. So what if you have to do the same old thing over and over again—you're alive and moving and beyond that you are loved so munificently that any rejection, any lasting depression is an affront to the giver of the gift of life itself.

REFLECTIONS ON LENT

Being in the desert . . .

EVEN those poets, travelers and mystics who profess to find beauty in the great deserts of the world admit that it is a terrible sort of splendor, an awe-invoking solitude of leafless harshness by day and a dome of limitless chill by night. One feels insignificant in the desert, not only scaled down to a speck by the dimensions of the vast horizon but because of the awful isolation. The desert cares nothing for prestige or power or talent; it speaks no words of praise, or consolation or love. It offers neither food nor drink. There is no small talk in the desert—not even from nature. It is one thing to go there to taste the silence in order to savor the fullness of life through contrast. It is a terrible thing to be forced to live there.

The Lenten season recalls the forty days which Jesus spent in the Judean wilderness, or desert, where he was tempted by Satan to abandon his mission in favor of power, personal comfort and wealth, or failing these things, simply in order to avoid his ordained passion and death. He repulsed these temptations and, spent and miserable, he was ministered to by God's angels and came out of the wilderness to begin his public life.

Even in biblical times and in a country which was largely wilderness, the desert was considered a fearful place. Potentially lethal by virtue of its heat and aridity, it was the refuge of outlaws and lepers, the home of snakes and scorpions, jackals and hyenas. Caravans in close company stuck to carefully plotted routes when they traversed the Sinai. Every well and oasis had a name. No one who could avoid it went alone into the desert and Jesus himself was no exception. Even Mark, writing years after the fact, knew that: "The Spirit *drove* Jesus out into the wilderness," he tells us.

For Jesus, the desert experience was not undertaken as repentance but as a test, a preparation, an experience of solitude in which he would be able to measure and accept the full import of the Father's will in his life and work. When he emerged he went into Galilee and began to preach repentance, as did John the Baptist before him: "The kingdom of God is close at hand."

Because of this, Lent is a season of repentance for Christians but it does not follow that we are to go into the desert to undertake this, either physically or spiritually. The desert remains a place very much to be avoided because it still symbolizes harshness, cruelty and isolation. In fact, if we are truly to repent, then we must examine our consciences first and foremost in the matter of how we have sinned. And in Jesus' own terms the greatest commandment is to love God with our whole hearts and our neighbor as ourselves. If we have failed to love God through acts of deliberate turning away, then let each of us account for that in our own hearts. But it may not be so simple to account for all the ways we have sinned against our neighbor.

It's quite easy to examine ourselves on this count and find little to disturb our complacency. We have killed no one, robbed no one, given scandal to none, cheated not a soul, borne no false witness. We have tried to mind our own business, perhaps even given some kind advice; and most certainly we have even been charitable to some and given a respectable amount of alms. We have, in short, observed both the letter and the spirit of the law—up to a point.

And that point is the dangerous one at which we feel justified and righteous. And who is to say if we are not, in fact, justified? No one can point the finger of accusation against us. It's only that what Jesus said about those who feel justified makes us a little uneasy. Perhaps repentance is not enough, or rather that repentance has a positive side as well.

If we do not feel we have to go into the desert to repent ourselves, perhaps it is our job to minister, like the angels did, to those who find themselves isolated in the modern deserts of our society—minister to them even if we do not feel any direct responsibility for putting them there; minister to them even if their own circumstances or weaknesses placed them there.

For there are many ways of being in the desert:

The old person living alone or in the crowded ward of a nursing home is in a desert.

The teen-ager lost in the peer pressures and confusions and emotional conflicts of modern society is in a desert.

The street people, the drug addicts, the homeless, the alcoholics who populate our cities are in a desert.

The divorced, the abandoned, the chronically or terminally ill are in a desert.

The immigrants, illegal aliens, and refugees of the world are in a desert.

Those in hopeless debt, in poverty and in the welfare cycle are in a desert.

The blind, the hard of hearing, the handicapped are in deserts.

Many of those who live in public housing projects are in deserts.

The housewife, the commuter, the assembly plant worker, the postal worker, the computer operator—almost all of us spend some part of our days in deserts.

Now it may seem a presumption of a different order to think of ourselves as ministering angels. But as Mark tells us the only company which Jesus found in the desert were the wild animals, so even if it is only as very limited, very human agents we can effectively intervene to help lessen the isolation and suffering of those many of us trapped in the deserts of modern society. It is the essence of the desert experience, the most debilitating part of it, to feel utterly alone, uncared for, insignificant, unrelievedly isolated, so that it is not the descent of a ministering angelic host one longs for, but simply the presence of another human being who understands, cares, and who may be able to help no more than that.

In Genesis God tells Noah, after the forty days and nights he and his family had spent riding out the flood—another kind of isolation—that he will place a rainbow in the sky as a sign of his covenant "between myself and every living creature with you for all generations." Noah's rainbow—God's rainbow—rose out of the waters and lit up the sky. It marked a return to life and an end to isolation. It was a signal both of God's forgiveness and of sinful humankind, and a promise that with his help we shall never have to endure the isolation of being cut off through sin from his promise of salvation and eternal life.

Even those trapped in the desert fall under the terms of that promise. But there is no water in the desert, no rainbow to be seen, unless it is reflected in the eyes of someone who cares enough to come out into the wilderness of other lives and share it.

Perhaps that is the form our repentance should take in these forty days of Lent—not only to reflect on the ways we have sinned but to drive ourselves into the deserts of some of the lives around us thereby ending the agony of isolation and bringing the good news of God's enduring promise of love.

PRACTICAL APPLICATION

It may be true that a smile costs nothing but it is not true that doing good costs the same. If we care to make this Lent a time of positive repentance by making a conscious effort to break into and thereby relieve the desert experience of one of our neighbors, friends or of strangers, then it will cost something in terms of personal commitment. It is not always easy to do good to others—especially those in modern desert experiences. We may have to bestir ourselves to find out just where and how our care can best be exercised. People in need often have built up protective barriers around themselves. They often live where we find it unpleasant or even frightening or depressing to go. At the very least, it means we will have to risk enduring some rebuffs or embarrassment. Deserts are not pleasant places to visit, much less live in. Nor should we offer our compassion and/or concrete help out of any expectation that we will be rewarded by a warm glow of self-satisfaction. But this should not deter us from making the effort. After all, repentance is still repentance.

REFLECTIONS ON THE PASSION ACCORDING TO MARK

Not being in control . . .

THE intensity of anxiety varies with the setting, but we all know the feelings of helplessness, frustration, fear, sometimes even despair which overtake us in situations where we have absolutely no control over what is happening—or could happen—to us. It can be in a hospital operating room as the anesthetist lowers the mask over our frightened eyes; it can be at 30,000 feet when the jet takes a sickening lurch that sends lunch trays and stomachs to the overhead; it can happen when a mother sees her first-born being swallowed up by the front door of an elementary school. As much and as often as we tell ourselves that there never really is a time when we are in complete control of our destinies we work constantly to be master of every situation that we can. Nobody likes to take chances with things that matter.

"Ecce homo!"—Behold the man!
In his remarkably crisp and dispassionate account of the passion and death of Jesus, Mark does not bother, as John does, to cite these words with which Pilate displayed the scourged and thorn-crowned Jesus to the crowd. Mark, in fact, has little interest in stirring up emotional reactions to these tragic and bloody events. He covers them much like a hardened modern newspaper reporter might have done. To him the important thing was to get down on record what happened to Jesus.
For a long time scholars thought that the Gospel of Mark

was simply an abbreviation of Matthew—whose name comes first in the ordering in which the Evangelists are named—because he left out things that Matthew used. But now all the experts are agreed that Mark's is the most primitive of the Gospels, as they say—the first to be written. Nobody goes so far as to insist that he was an eye-witness to the events he records so brusquely here, but the possibility cannot be totally ruled out. There's that curious mention of the young man who followed Jesus after his arrest on the Mount of Olives, the one who was wearing only a linen cloth. When the guards tried to take him along by force he pulled free and ran naked into the night. There are those who conjecture that Mark would include this—for him—highly extraneous bit of color only because he was the young man in question.

But even though Mark does not use the words *Ecce homo*, the Jesus he gives to us is indeed very much a man. A man who, though surely visible now to the reader who believes as the Son of God, is also just a man, a human being.

Human beings are not able, as Jesus was, to look into their own futures and see the suffering which awaits them. They are not able to tell their friends just who and what they will encounter when they go into the city as Jesus did when he made arrangements for his entry into Jerusalem and for the Last Supper. But gods don't admit to great distress and throw themselves on the ground as Jesus did, nor permit themselves to be captured, humiliated, tried and tortured—not, that is, unless they are as human as is the Jesus which Mark is at pains to show us.

And one of the chief ways in which Mark accomplishes his dual purpose of revealing both the human and divine aspects of Jesus is to make it clear that Jesus surrendered himself completely to the will of the Father. Surrendering to this will meant giving up control—all control—of his destiny. From the moment the Last Supper ends and the Passion begins, things happen *to* Jesus, he does not cause them to happen. But the terrible thing was that he knew—as Son of God—precisely what was going to happen.

In his lack of control he was very much like us when we feel anxiety and fear in situations in which we can do nothing to help ourselves or those we love. But at least we, in our ignorance of the future, can cling to the hope, however frail and fleeting, that things may actually turn out for the best. Jesus did not have even the luxury of unfounded hope to cushion his dread. "My soul is sorrowful to the point of death," he tells the confused disciples. By repetition of the waking and sleeping of these witnesses, Mark makes it clear that there was far more to the passion of Jesus than mere physical pain. He went through a form of psychological hell that was uniquely awful.

In this light, the reproach he gives Peter about staying awake and praying not to be put to the test because "the spirit is willing but the flesh is weak" can almost be seen as self-recrimination, an admonishment to his own too human flesh to match the strength of purpose required to completely turn over control of its well-being to the will of God.

So when we read Mark's account from this perspective it is certainly an account of what was happening to Jesus, but it is also an account with which we, as fellow humans, should easily be able to enter into and empathize with. It was not some Promethean being, some divine mirage who could by a whim of will cut himself off from pain, abandonment, desolation, whom Mark would have us see nailed to the cross—it is a human being made of tender flesh and coursing blood like us. Mark wants us to know to what full and awful extent Jesus did in fact suffer for us; that he suffered not just in atonement but in place of all of us so that we might not ever have to fear the ultimate results of being out of control of our eternal destiny.

PRACTICAL APPLICATION

Thanks to the passion and death of Jesus we, who truly and faithfully believe that he is the Son of God, our human brother who is yet that same divine son, have been given the assurance that our mutual Father has taken control of our ultimate destiny. So, however much we continue to exhibit our very human fear about losing control of our ability to protect ourselves and our loved ones, our anxiety about situations in which we are totally in the ·hands of circumstances, we should rejoice that we are in the best of hands when it comes to what is truly most important about our lives. Even when we panic and run naked into the night of fear as did the young disciple who followed Jesus after his arrest, we are assured that we can come safely home again, guided by the light that Jesus brought into the darkness of the world.

REFLECTIONS ON EASTER

Hearing incredibly good news . . .

IN the early hours of the morning the phone rings. A voice on the other end, sounding dim and far away but very, very excited tells you . . . . What? The best thing you could possibly expect to hear. Something so good, in fact, that you never expected to hear it. Something so good that you can't believe it. You've won the Nobel Prize . . . the Heisman Trophy . . . the State Lottery . . . a trip around the world . . . whatever, it's something mind-boggling.

So how do you react? By saying "That's nice! Thank you very much for calling"? No, your head starts to spin. Adrenalin flows through your veins like water through a fire hose. "I can't believe it!" you shout. Or, "You've got to be kidding!" You continue to refuse to believe news so impossibly great. Your mind resists being tricked and disappointed as it has on thousands of other occasions when false hopes crashed onto the rock of realism. You beg for reassurance, for clarification. And even when the caller swears to cross his heart and hope to die if what he's saying isn't true, you still resist belief.

Can you hear the cry, coming just before daybreak on a morning nearly two thousand years ago now?

Is the voice so faint that you can scarcely hear it or does it resound close and bright in your ear?

Does its message fill your heart with unbearable joy and gladness or does it merely remind you of something you've heard so many times that you've grown indifferent and blase?

Is it such good news that you can scarcely believe it or is it something so incredible that you refuse to believe it any longer?

It is, to be sure, a farfetched thing that the Easter gospel expects us to swallow—that a man dead for three days came back to life, escaped the tight layers of his burial shroud, pushed back the stone that sealed this tomb and disappeared. Nothing that the gospel tells us offers conclusive proof of the resurrection of Jesus of Nazareth. Grave robbing was not uncommon—you never knew what treasure might be wrapped up inside a shroud—a ring, a gold chain. No, an empty tomb and discarded burial clothes prove nothing in themselves. Nor does the testimony of a bunch of wild-eyed grieving women who loved the deceased; nor that of the deceased's disciples, who had a very large axe to grind by claiming that their leader was brought back to life through the power of the God whose Son he claimed to be.

Yet the events set down by John about the first Easter morning have been and are believed by millions, alive and dead. Believed most fervently even though never witnessed. Believed as the greatest good news of all times. Believed because these people chose to believe, wanted to believe. And we who are here today count ourselves among that number.

It was, I think, the novelist Anthony Burgess who wrote that whenever he grew skeptical about the veracity of the Gospel accounts of the resurrection he went back and read John's account of it. To Burgess's professional writer's eye one line stands out: "They ran together, but the other disciple, running faster than Peter, reached the tomb first." That, says Burgess, is a detail that no one intent on merely contriving a story would think the least bit necessary to include.

And it is this faster disciple, the one Jesus loved, that we should all try to emulate. John says that when he entered the empty tomb and saw the burial cloths he believed. John does not say the same of Peter. Peter, also came to believe in the fact of the resurrection, but the other disciple was the *first* to believe. It was this same beloved disciple—who presumably reciprocated this special affection Jesus had for him—who is earlier credited as being the first to recognize Jesus on the shore of the Sea of Tiberius. At the tomb he saw no more than Mary Magdalen and Peter, but he did not hesitate to believe, nor did he allow himself to be distracted by all the other possible explanations for a missing corpse. Unlike his fellow disciple Thomas, he believed without seeing. His love for Jesus gave him the special gift of faith. He is being held up here by John as the model follower of Christ—an example for us all.

The promise of Easter, the incredible good news of the resurrection of Jesus, is that all who believe in him will have eternal life. All we have to do to merit this gift is to believe and follow him—but the belief must *first be there* and it must come, not from any practical or scientific or historical proof, but through the grace of God and bestowed through our open love for Jesus.

We who share in that promise, who love Jesus and try to follow him with the fullness of love for him, ourselves and our neighbors, now celebrate this greatest and best of news with the psalmist when he sings:

This is the day the Lord has made;
Let us rejoice and be glad.

PRACTICAL APPLICATION

Our reaction to incredibly good news shares something in common with our reaction to terribly bad news. After we have brought ourselves to accept the reality of either, most people say: "What did I do to deserve this?" In some cases we can actually find some reasons why we do, in fact, deserve what we have gotten. But in the case of the greatest good news of all—the gift of everlasting life by God—we really can claim to have done nothing to deserve it. But the least we can do is accept it under the terms it was given, as an utterly gracious act of love on the part of God. This acceptance entails believing in the giver with our whole hearts and following the commandments of love communicated to us in the life and death of his son. The two are inseparably connected so that there cannot be one without the other. So to refuse to believe the good news is, in effect, not to receive the gift. To take it for granted, to treat it with indifference and skepticism, to treat it as something too often heard to make much difference in our lives, is to throw the gift back into the face of the risen Christ. Let us run to accept it, run as fast as the disciple whom Jesus loved, to accept it with open arms on Easter morning.

REFLECTIONS ON PENTECOST

Experiencing the unseeable . . .

WHEN the wind stirs the leaves of the elm or sends a gentle riff across an otherwise tranquil lake we know it is present though we cannot see it. X-Rays reveal unseeable defects in both bones and metal. Ultra-sound does the same deep in human tissue. The air is filled with invisible forces that we cannot detect until we turn on our television or radio sets and enjoy the miracle of sound, pictures and color. And sometimes, staring at the night sky it is the opposite that is true. We "see" and experience the light from a star billions of miles away but which is no longer really where it appears to be, having long since spent the energy which we perceive and burned itself out. The skilled magician can also make us believe we have seen what we have not and just as readily not see what in fact is there. Our sense of reality is limited to dimensions that let us comprehend "all that is" as through a glass darkly.

Fifty days after Passover the Jews celebrated Pentecost Day in commemoration of the handing down of the commandments—the law—to Moses from God on Mount Sinai. We associate that event also with the forging of the Brazen Calf, the false god, which the faithless Israelites worshipped while Moses was on the mountain. In today's reading from Acts we find the disciples once again gathered in a room—waiting for the gift, the power which Jesus had promised to send them. Suddenly the Holy Spirit descends with the sound of rushing wind and in living flames. Where once their forefathers had assembled to adore a visible but lifeless idol, the disciples now experienced the powerful breath of an invisible but living God. There is no breath in graven images.

What the disciples felt precisely we cannot know, but they evidently became very animated and began to speak in strange tongues so that those who gathered in the streets in response to the mighty sound which filled the whole house —a sound that presumably made itself heard not to the whole city but in the hearts of all "devout" people—thought that the disciples were overly full of "new wine." This gift of tongues made it possible for the disciples to make themselves understood in every language. What sounded like gibberish to Jewish ears made perfect sense to Parthians, Medes and Mesopotamians. And we are immediately reminded of another Old Testament story turned on its ear.

Just as the New Pentecost becomes a feast of the Spirit of God rather than a commemoration of the Law of God, so it became the time when the confusion of languages brought about by God's wrath at the prideful people who built the Tower of Babel is lifted so that all can hear the Good News of salvation through Jesus, the risen Christ.

And that is the meaning of Pentecost which we might focus on here. The coming of the Holy Spirit—to the disciples, and to all who came after them—makes it possible to hear the word of God with ears blocked by purely human concerns and hearts choked with the weeds of self-interest and absorption. Those who heard the Good News for the first time that Pentecost day experienced the true miracle, not just of the Gift of Tongues, but of God's love for all humankind for all ages. How marvelous, we say, to have witnessed such an event, to have heard those words and voices.

But, as Father Patrick J. Brennan points out in his new book *Spirituality for an Anxious Age* [Thomas More Press], the wonder of that Pentecostal experience is still alive in our own day: "That word is being spoken to us often in our own deep memory, in our conscience, in our unconscious, in our imagination, in our own thoughts and feelings. God's Word takes on a variety of shapes and forms. Sometimes we receive a word of challenge. At other times, the word is comforting. Still other times the word is indicting. Often the word is healing and reconciling."

The marvel is, writes Father Brennan, that "the Word of God is spoken to us each day as really as it was to the great heroes and heroines of Scripture. In this age of 'hurry sickness,' we have dulled our perceptive abilities. The Word goes ignored or unheard. The person of faith who is trying to become a deep listener gradually realizes that one cannot seriously listen to self without beginning to listen to God also."

On the first Pentecost the Spirit announced its coming in sound and fire. Today its presence is still with us but it speaks in a quiet voice in a language that can be understood by all people of good will and devotion to the love of God. It is a voice which we must still our hearts and whirling heads to hear. And hear it we must if we are to have life.

PRACTICAL APPLICATION

One definition of the word spirit is "the principle of life and vital activity." No one can see spirit but it would be foolish to doubt that each of us is possessed of just such a principle of life and vital activity. To gaze upon a corpse is to know that something has departed that was surely there. Just so, the Holy Spirit of Pentecost might be named "the principle of divine life and activity." And it is just as impossible to see the Holy Spirit as it is to see a human spirit. And it is just as foolish to doubt its presence and reality on those grounds as it is to doubt the reality of our own spirit.

Yet, because we do have the Holy Spirit with us still as a consequence of the first Pentecost, perhaps there is a way, with the help of that same Spirit to whom all things are possible, to experience the unseeable.

At the conclusion of Ray Bradbury's science fiction classic *The Martian Chronicles* there is a memorable scene. A family of colonizing earthlings stands amid the ruins of what had once been a great civilization on the Red Planet. The father alone knows that aside from his family the planet is now devoid of life. He asks his wife and children if they would like to see some Martians. Curious, half-frightened, terribly excited, they follow him to a parapet overlooking a wide and placid canal. Lie down, the father tells them, and gaze deeply into the water. They do so and he tosses in a stone. As the ripples subside they are gradually able to make out the ever-clearing mirror images of their own faces. "There!" the father tells them, "there are the Martians!"

And so it may be for us. If we are determined to catch a glimpse of the Holy Spirit today, the best way to do so is to look into the mirror of our eyes and into the eyes of those good people about us whom we love and who love us in return. There, in that animated light of Christian love, one for the other, that is where to see the Holy Spirit in the full glory of his Divine, living, vital reality.